Razor-Wire Secrets: The Hidden War

"The gripping true account of one man's fight for survival in a world of treachery and terrorism."

Rusty Le Grande

All rights reserved. No part of this publication may be reproduced, stored in a retrieval system or transmitted in any form by any means, electronic, mechanical, photocopying, recording or otherwise, without the prior written permission of the publishers and copyright holders.

The moral right of the author has been asserted.

Copyright © Rusty Le Grande 2019

Cover design with elements from Canva

Printed and bound in Australia by Ingram Spark

ISBN: 978-1-7641087-0-6

Foreword

In a world fraught with uncertainty and tension, the years following the dawn of the twenty-first century brought about a seismic shift in the global landscape. The echoes of the 9/11 attacks reverberated across continents, instilling a palpable sense of fear and urgency in cities once thought invulnerable. Australia, a land renowned for its tranquillity, found itself uncomfortably positioned in the crosshairs of a rising tide of extremism. The Bali bombings of 2002 further shattered our collective sense of safety, waking us from a complacent slumber and heralding an era defined by vigilance and the spectre of terrorism. Amidst this turmoil, a personal journey unfolded—a journey steeped in the complexities of identity, duty, and moral quandary.

I am Rusty Legrande, a name chosen to shield my true identity, but the story that follows is one that demands authenticity. It is a narrative woven from the threads of my upbringing in a loving, hardworking family, a family that had once sought refuge in the embrace of Australia after fleeing the political unrest of the Middle East. My father, once a diplomat, transformed into a revered elder within our community, navigating the shifting sands of a new life while instilling values of integrity and resilience in his six children. But as the world outside grew darker,

I found myself grappling with questions of loyalty, fear, and a longing to serve.

My family's legacy of service took an unexpected turn when I was approached to undertake a role that would forever alter the course of my life. The Australian intelligence community recognized my unique background—my Middle Eastern heritage, my fluency in Arabic, and my prior experience as a teacher within the prison system. I was asked to infiltrate local Islamic community groups suspected of harbouring extremist ideologies, a task laden with peril and ethical dilemmas. It was not simply a job; it was a call to arms, a chance to protect my country and the values I held dear.

As I embarked on this undercover mission, the gravity of my decision weighed heavily on my conscience. The stakes were high, not only for me but for my family, who remained blissfully unaware of the danger I was about to plunge into. The clandestine world I was entering was fraught with betrayal, suspicion, treachery, and violence. I would be walking a tightrope among individuals whose ideologies clashed violently with my own—individuals who would stop at nothing to achieve their goals.

My assignment took an unexpected and harrowing turn when high-profile members of a terrorist group, led by a notorious cleric known only as Abdul NB, were arrested, leaving a power vacuum and a sense of urgency in the air. The need for intelligence was paramount; I had to go deeper into the heart of the prison system, where the most dangerous minds were confined. The challenge of surviving within that hostile environment, surrounded by murderers, paedophiles, and the most violent criminals, became a reality I could not escape.

Every day was a battle for survival; the constant threat of exposure loomed over me like a dark cloud. As a clean-skin—someone with no criminal history—I was an enigma to the hardened inmates. Some suspected I was a plant, an undercover cop, and I had to remain vigilant, adapting to the ever-changing dynamics of the prison hierarchy. The razor-sharp tension of those moments is something words can scarcely capture.

As I navigated the bleak corridors of the Victorian prison system, I witnessed firsthand the atrocious conditions that bred despair and violence. The walls, cloaked in a history of sorrow and rage, told tales of lives lost to the darkness. Within that environment, I was not merely a participant; I became an observer of human nature at its most raw and unfiltered.

The choices I made during those two years of undercover work were not without sacrifice. They demanded an immense toll on my psyche, challenging my beliefs and reshaping my identity. The impact on my family was profound; a veil of secrecy shrouded my life, creating distances that I feared might never be bridged.

This book is not merely a recounting of my experiences; it is a testament to the complexities of duty, the price of courage, and the indomitable spirit of those who dare to stand against the tide of hatred. It is a story of resilience in the face of adversity and a call to understand the shadows that lurk in our communities. As you turn the pages, I invite you to step into my world—a world defined by treachery, survival, and the relentless pursuit of truth. This is not just my story; it is a narrative that echoes the struggles of many who walk the fine line between right and wrong in a world that often blurs the lines of morality. Prepare yourself for a journey that is as enlightening as it is harrowing, where every revelation leads to deeper questions about justice, loyalty, and the human condition. Welcome to my story, a chronicle of my life undercover, and the tumultuous journey that changed me forever.

Dedication

This book is dedicated to the memory of my father, a man who refused to let poverty and adversity extinguish his spirit. He taught us invaluable lessons, reminding us that even with very little, we still had so much to cherish. My father often said, "Poverty can kill a person, but prosperity can do so, too." He emphasized the importance of looking to those who make enduring commitments, regardless of their circumstances. He would remind us, "There's more to life than who dies with the most toys." Yet, the greatest lesson he imparted was that the true measure of a man lies in how well he provides for his children. While my father bestowed upon me countless insights about life, no one could ever teach me the lessons I learned from my greatest hero, my beautiful son. His spirit and resilience during the most challenging times have filled me with immense pride. To my wonderful friends and family who stood by me in my hour of need—without your unwavering love, support, and encouragement, I would not be here today to share this story. Thank you to all of you; you know who you are.

Table of Contents

Foreword 3

Dedication 7

Chapter 1 - When Winning Means Losing 10

Chapter 2 - Mainstream vs. Shadow: The Fine Line 15

Chapter 3 - Inside the Metropolitan Assessment Prison (MAP) 20

Chapter 4 - The Reality of the Metropolitan Remand Centre (MRC) 25

Chapter 5 - Living with Paranoia Behind Bars 30

Chapter 6 - Trust and Treachery: The Unwritten Rule 37

Chapter 7- Charlotte & The Spine: Allies or Adversaries? ... 44

Chapter 8- Secrets of the Cell: What Stays Behind Bars 50

Chapter 9- The Prison Merry-Go-Round: No Escape 55

Chapter 10- Tommy C and Frankie B: The Oddities of Jail . 59

Chapter 11- Road Trips Through Confinement 64

Chapter 12- Drugs, Medication, and Control in the Jail System 69

Chapter 13- The Phantom Shitter: Tales of the Unseen 74

Chapter 14: Whispers of Danger: Gathering Intel 79

Chapter 15- The Final Road Trip: The Betrayal Lingers 84

Chapter16- Open Camp or Total Chaos? 91

Chapter 17- The Bombay Cabbie: Culinary Comforts in Chaos 97

Chapter 18- Release and the Post-Prison Struggle 104

Chapter 19- Turning Trials into Triumphs 109

Chapter 20- Lessons from Loss: Embracing the Journey... 113

Chapter 21- Footprints of Failure and Success 117

Chapter 22- Resilience in the Face of Adversity 121

Chapter 23- If It Is To Be, It's Up To Me: Taking Charge.. 125

Final Statement 129

Author's Note on Naming Individuals 132

Poems from My Journey 135

    The Nights Are So Lonely 136

    22 Hour Lockdown 138

    Doing Time 141

    Until Forever 143

    Another Day in Paradise 144

    Another Day In Jail 146

    Away From My Love 148

    Jail Is Not Fun 149

Attachments and Sketches 151

Chapter 1 - When Winning Means Losing

To learn, you must want to be taught.

Jail is not easy, nor should it be. Each of us ends up behind bars for a reason—a reason we often struggle to confront. But for me, my circumstances are not what they seem. I didn't come here by choice or as a result of my own actions; I was placed in this environment as part of an elaborate undercover operation aimed at gathering intelligence on dangerous individuals. My mission is clear: to work from the inside and help ensure the safety of my community and country.

While I underwent rigorous training and preparation for over two years prior to this assignment, nothing could have fully equipped me for the harsh realities of prison life—the deceit, treachery, and lies that permeate these walls. To gain entry into the prison system, a carefully crafted back-story was developed. I was placed here under the guise of having committed white-collar fraud, a narrative that would be easier for the other inmates to accept. I portrayed myself as a man who had succumbed to a gambling addiction, a vice that supposedly led me to make poor choices and ultimately commit a crime to support my habit. While the facade may have its roots in truth, it serves a greater purpose.

I understand that I have choices, and I am old enough to know better. I am blessed with a loving family, particularly my wonderful wife, who stands by me through thick and thin. She embodies loyalty, hard work, and dedication—a brilliant mother to our son. I have no excuses; I am loved and supported. Yet here I am, immersed in this complex mission, navigating the murky waters of prison life and the shadows of those I must observe.

While I maintain this pretence, I am also acutely aware of the gravity of my task. I must gather intelligence on the individuals inside, including potential threats and activities that could harm our society. As I engage with the inmates, I focus not only on blending in but also on gathering vital information that could prevent tragedies.

Throughout this journey, I've reflected on my role and the painful truths that accompany it. I know that my wife and son are outside, grappling with their own challenges while I am here, all in the name of a greater good. It's a bittersweet reality—my presence in jail is a sacrifice for the safety of others, yet it weighs heavily on my heart.

While I am committed to my mission, my thoughts often drift to my family. My wife, in particular, has been my anchor throughout this harrowing journey. I am grateful for her unwavering support, even as she navigates the fallout of my decision to become part of this operation. Many women might have walked away in her position, but she chose to stand by me, showcasing her remarkable loyalty, strength and compassion.

The irony of having a loving family while being incarcerated makes this experience even more challenging. If I had only myself to worry about, I could focus solely on my mission. But knowing my family struggles with the consequences of my actions adds an emotional burden I carry with me. Each phone call and letter becomes a lifeline, grounding me in reality and reminding me of the stakes involved.

Many inmates receive no letters or phone calls, a heartbreaking reality that underscores the isolation of prison life. I have been fortunate to receive a deluge of messages from my wife, which help me feel connected and supported. Writing back has become a therapeutic outlet, allowing me to process my thoughts and emotions as I navigate this complex world.

In the grand scheme of things, my role in this undercover operation is not as straightforward as many might think. I am not here to serve time for my own crimes; rather, I am here to uncover the truth about the individuals around me.

As I observe the other inmates, I realize that we share a commonality—each of us has made choices that led us here, but my choices serve a different purpose.

While I may share a cell with men who have committed heinous acts, my mission compels me to confront the reality of those actions without losing sight of my goals. I am not seeking sympathy; I am embracing my reality as an operative working to protect my community.

The environment in jail is rife with deception and manipulation. Many inmates alter their narratives, presenting their crimes in a more socially acceptable light. The truth often surfaces, and those who attempt to hide their past find themselves facing the consequences. I've seen firsthand how lies can unravel, exposing individuals who thought they could escape accountability.

As I navigate this intricate world behind bars, I recognize that my journey is one of many. We all have our flaws, and while the choices that led us here may differ, the need for accountability remains universal. I am a product of my decisions, and now I must find a way to reconcile my past with the man I aspire to be.

Ultimately, my experience in prison has taught me that while we may win some battles, the war against ignorance and violence continues long after we exit those razor-wire gates. I may have stumbled into this world, but I refuse to let my past define me. Instead, I aim to learn and grow from it, forging a path toward a safer future for all.

Chapter 2 - Mainstream vs. Shadow: The Fine Line

When you choose the behaviour, you choose the consequences!

I must admit that I was incredibly naive before stepping into the world of incarceration. Like most outsiders, I thought all jails were essentially the same, merely divided into high security and medium security. I had no real understanding of what to expect behind those imposing walls. As the time approached for my mission, I was acutely aware of the precision and detail taken to orchestrate my entry into the Custody Centre. The timing was critical, and the process was delicate yet expertly executed by my handlers and the intelligence services team. While I won't divulge the specifics of how it was done, I can say that once I was planted inside, I had to be ready to begin my mission.

Jail is certainly no fun, and it shouldn't be. It is the most degrading, dehumanizing, demoralizing, and shattering experience one could imagine. Once you enter, you lose your identity. They refer to you by your last name or your CRN (criminal record number), stripping away any sense of individuality you once had. Each day serves as a reminder that you are just a number, a cog in a relentless machine designed to dismantle your humanity.

As I navigated this new reality, I was acutely aware of my undercover mission. I had to maintain my façade as a white-collar criminal, a man whose gambling addiction propelled him into a life of fraud. Every interaction was a careful dance, blending in with the other inmates while constantly fearing exposure. If they discovered who I truly was, my life could be forfeit.

Upon arrival, I quickly realized that there were no clear instructions about jail procedures or rules. I was left in blissful ignorance, forced to seek out information while grappling with the overwhelming urge to remain inconspicuous. Asking too many questions of the other inmates could invite suspicion, and I was determined to avoid drawing attention to myself.

My time at the Custody Centre was a nightmare. Although I was only there for a week, the living conditions were horrific. I lost eight kilograms in that short span, a testament to the psychological toll it took on me. The experience was shocking, and even now, the memory of those days remains etched in my mind. It was a place that felt like a prison within a prison, a low point that I never wanted to revisit.

The layout of the Custody Centre was confining. I was placed in C Yard with about 18 other inmates, crammed into a small space that felt more like a holding pen than a facility for rehabilitation. The walls felt as if they were closing in on me, and the lack of privacy was suffocating. Each morning, our cell doors would be flung open at 6:30 a.m., and we were herded into the Yard like cattle, forced to spend the entire day in that claustrophobic environment.

Showering became a public spectacle, a stark reminder of the vulnerability that accompanies incarceration. There was only one toilet, a grim reality that stripped us of any semblance of dignity. I found it hard to fathom how I would survive this experience while keeping my secret intact. Each moment felt fraught with the risk of exposure, and I had to be on guard at all times.

As I settled into the Custody Centre, I quickly discerned the pecking order among the inmates. The weak were often preyed upon, with stronger individuals standing over them for cigarettes or other personal items. To survive, I knew I had to project strength, to send a message that I wouldn't be an easy target. My cellmate David would later tell me the importance of standing up for myself; it was a lesson I would carry with me as I navigated this treacherous environment.

One of the most unforgettable aspects of my time at the Custody Centre was the appalling quality of the food. Each meal was a reminder of my new reality. Breakfast consisted of a piece of toast and a small sachet of jam, while lunch was a meager salad that left much to be desired. I couldn't stomach the evening meals, which were often a watery mess heated in a microwave. I found it nearly impossible to eat, and the weight loss only compounded my feelings of despair.

During my time in the Custody Centre, I was at my absolute lowest. The psychological effects of my experiences still lingered. I had encountered violence in the past, an unexpected attack from a young inmate high on drugs. The memory of that night haunted me, further eroding my sense of safety. By the time I arrived at the Custody Centre, I was on edge, fully aware that my life had taken a devastating turn.

In this bleak setting, where I felt utterly helpless, I was trapped in a cage with 20 other men, unable to reach out for support or communicate with the outside world. The feeling of despair was stifling, and I grappled with the thought that I might never escape this nightmare. I was fortunate to be there for only eight days, but the experience of confinement was soul-crushing.

Amid the darkness, the only glimmer of hope came from the 'Sisters' who visited a few times a week. Their brief presence provided a much-needed connection to the outside world, even if only for a few moments. While their ability to assist was limited, their willingness to listen offered a flicker of solace in an otherwise oppressive environment. I would forever be grateful for the compassion they extended to those of us who felt so lost.

As I continued my undercover mission, I remained acutely aware of the stakes involved. Each day was a balancing act, a tightrope walk between maintaining my cover and navigating the perilous world of prison life. In an environment rife with hostility, I had to find a way to survive, to gather the insights I needed for my task while keeping my true identity hidden. The fear of being outed loomed large, but as I settled into my role, I steeled myself for the journey ahead.

Chapter 3 - Inside the Metropolitan Assessment Prison (MAP)

The good you do today will be forgotten tomorrow. Do good anyway.

After spending 7-8 days at the Custody Centre, I was transferred to the Melbourne Assessment Prison (MAP). This was my first true experience in a real jail, and I quickly realized just how unprepared I was for the harsh realities that awaited me. Located near the Telstra Dome, I had driven past the MAP countless times, but now, it stood before me as a harbinger of my new life—a life filled with fear and uncertainty.

Upon arrival, I endured the typical processing: a shower, a strip search, and a uniform issued with little regard for my dignity. As I was led by an officer to my assigned unit, I was still reeling from the chaos of the Custody Centre. In a moment of weakness, I made a rookie mistake. As the officer opened the glass door for me, I instinctively said, "Thanks mate." The officer's furious response shattered my fragile state of mind: "I'm not your fucken mate! You call me Sir or Mr! Don't ever call me mate, you piece of fucken shit!" I quickly learned that in this world, respect is demanded, not given, and the rules are unforgiving.

Once I stepped into 'Unit 4', I was placed in a double cell with a man named David. Standing at 6'3", he was an imposing figure, but he appeared friendly enough. Internally, I was terrified, but I knew that showing fear could lead to disastrous consequences. David had spent a decade at Pentridge and had stories that were both fascinating and alarming. As I listened, I absorbed his advice on survival: "You trust nobody, and you do your jail." His words echoed in my mind as I navigated this new reality, constantly aware that my mission required me to blend in while keeping my true purpose hidden.

The MAP was a pressure cooker of tensions, filled with inmates on edge, many of whom were on remand. Just days into my stay, the chaos escalated. I witnessed not one, but three brutal fights break out in quick succession, each more violent than the last. The first was a savage brawl over a perceived slight, resulting in one inmate getting slashed with a makeshift weapon. The second erupted when a group of men cornered another inmate, delivering a flurry of punches that left him gasping on the floor. The third was a bloodbath, a stabbing that left a man bleeding out in the yard, a gruesome spectacle that sent shockwaves through the unit. The graphic nature of these events sent chills down my spine and served as a stark reminder of the stakes at play.

In the midst of this turmoil, I was confronted with the horrifying sight of an inmate in the cell across from me being bashed within an inch of his life. I watched as he lay there, battered and barely conscious, while the chaos continued around us. I saw everything but saw nothing. In prison, nobody ever sees anything. I knew that if I was to survive, I had to turn a blind eye to the brutality surrounding me. This was just business, and I understood that all too well. I had been trained for these situations; I just never anticipated how quickly they would come.

Lockdown hours at the MAP were from 4:30 PM until 9:30 AM the next day, meaning we were confined for 17 hours each day. We were allowed out for only 7 hours, which included breakfast at 9:30 AM, lunch at 12 noon, and dinner at 4 PM. This was not ideal, but this was prison. During my first few nights with David, he reiterated the importance of standing your ground. "The first time somebody tries to stand over you, don't let them. If you do, you're fucked!" I took his advice to heart, knowing that if my cover was to remain intact, I had to project strength. I had to stay close to my potential targets, especially the Muslim brothers and other extremists, who were everywhere but nowhere at the same time. My job was to start my work, find them, and earn their trust.

The cells were filthy and reeked of body odour and stale urine. With barely enough space to breathe, I quickly acclimated to my surroundings. I had a small toilet with no seat, a basin, and a mouldy shower. Despite the horrendous conditions, my focus remained on my mission. Writing letters became my escape; it was a way to maintain contact with my loved ones while also documenting my experiences. I poured my feelings of guilt and remorse into those pages, desperately trying to stay connected to the person I once was.

As the days passed, I felt the intense scrutiny of the atmosphere. Every chat, every glance was loaded with tension and the unspoken understanding of the violence that could erupt at any moment. I was in a mainstream facility, and violence was a common occurrence. The atmosphere was thick with the threat of chaos, and I had to navigate this minefield carefully, always aware of the personalities around me.

I continued to write letters, desperate to stay connected to my family and friends. Each letter was a lifeline, a way to express my thoughts and feelings while maintaining my cover. I realized that perceptions change dramatically once you're behind bars, and I had to brace myself for the possible abandonment by those I once considered friends.

Through it all, I held onto the belief that I could survive this ordeal. I would not let fear dictate my actions; instead, I would embrace my mission. I was in this for my country, and I refused to let the darkness of this world extinguish the light of my purpose.

Chapter 4 - The Reality of the Metropolitan Remand Centre (MRC)

You are spending life! Every day you've wasted is a day you'll never get back again.

After 4-5 weeks at the Melbourne Assessment Prison (MAP), a sudden knock on my cell door jolted me awake. "Pack your bags... you're on the escort list, you've got 10 minutes!" the officer barked. Anxiety surged through me as I quickly stuffed my few belongings into a plastic bag. Just as I was beginning to settle into the routines of MAP, I was being uprooted once again. The relentless cycle of movement left me feeling powerless, as though my life was no longer my own. Questions swirled in my mind, but I knew better than to ask the officers for explanations. Compliance was key; defiance could lead to a Minor Offense Report or worse.

The senior officer escorted me and a couple of other inmates to the administration area, where we were ordered to stand on a white line and wait silently. I couldn't shake the feeling of being just another pawn in this unforgiving game. As I stood there, I sensed the eyes of seasoned inmates on me, their curiosity mingling with suspicion. My arrival had sparked interest, a threat to the status quo.

Long-timers watched me closely, their paranoia palpable; a newbie like me aroused suspicion, and I had to be on my toes. One slipup could be fatal.

Upon arrival at the Metropolitan Remand Centre (MRC), a maximum-security facility touted as the latest "state-of-the-art" prison, I steeled myself for what lay ahead. After the usual checks and a brief chat with a psych nurse, I was subjected to the humiliating indignity of a strip search. The experience hit me like a punch to the gut, and I couldn't help but wonder how my life had spiraled into this nightmare.

As I entered the MRC, I was thrust into a pressure cooker of tension. The facility was half-full with 296 inmates, and I could only imagine the chaos that came with such overcrowding. On my third day, I witnessed the harrowing consequences of that chaos firsthand. An argument erupted over a phone call—a coveted privilege in this hellhole—leading to an Asian inmate plunging a sharpened pencil, fashioned into a deadly shiv, into another inmate's neck. Blood shot up in the air, splattering against the walls as the victim fell to the ground. I was frozen, horrified by the brutality. Officers rushed in, but the other inmates remained unfazed, as if this was just another day in the jungle. I later learned that the stabbed inmate succumbed to his injuries. The attacker, I discovered, was on a murder charge for killing his brother, making it clear that if he was willing to kill his own flesh and blood, he wouldn't hesitate to kill over a phone breach.

While in Admissions, I glanced at the whiteboard in the supervisor's office: "Muster 296." I knew that meant there were 296 prisoners at the MRC that day. The atmosphere felt charged, and I knew I had to navigate this minefield carefully. The Attwood Unit was a rectangular area with cells lined on two tiers, and the atmosphere felt more civilized. I was relieved to be in a space where the officers were approachable, and my strategy of remaining respectful and polite paid off. It was crucial for me to maintain my undercover role, and I knew that any hint of aggression or hostility could jeopardize my mission.

As I settled into my routine, I began to observe the dynamics of the prison. The MRC was a melting pot of personalities, and I quickly learned that I had to stay vigilant. I kept my head down, avoiding involvement in the petty politics that often led to violence. I was acutely aware that one misstep could lead to exposure, and I was determined to remain undetected while gathering information on my targets.

After a week in Attwood, I was moved to the Cambridge Unit in C-Yard. The daily routines were more civilized; lockdowns occurred at 6 PM on weekdays and 7 PM on weekends, offering a reprieve from the gruelling schedules of the MAP. But beneath the surface, tensions were brewing. Lorenzo, one of my new cell-mates, was a junkie dealing drugs right out of our cottage. I had never touched drugs in my life, and the thought of being associated with his activities made my skin crawl. I was acutely aware that if he got caught, we would all be implicated.

As days passed, the flow of traffic into our cottage increased, and it became glaringly obvious that Lorenzo's activities were drawing attention. He was on a murder charge, awaiting an appeal, and his indifference to the consequences of his actions was maddening. I had to remind myself that I was in a world defined by survival of the fittest, and I needed to keep my distance from the chaos.

Despite the turmoil, I knew I had to establish important relationships with the Muslim brothers and targets within the prison. Their weekly prayer sessions became my entry point, granting me access to individuals who were both good and bad. I needed to glean as much evidence and information as I could to provide our state and national law enforcement and intelligence agencies with what they needed. After all, this was why I was here.

The next weeks were challenging as I faced the consequences of Lorenzo's actions. I was tainted by association, and the isolation I felt was unbearable. Even though I had remained clean, the stigma lingered. I couldn't shake the feeling that I was under constant scrutiny, and my resolve to maintain my cover and continue my mission felt more precarious than ever.

Through it all, I clung to the belief that I could navigate this treacherous landscape. I needed to stay focused on my mission, gathering information while remaining undetected. Every day was a battle for survival, but I was resolute in my determination not to let the darkness consume me. In a place where trust was a luxury I could not afford, I had to tread carefully, always aware that one misstep could lead to dire consequences.

Chapter 5 - Living with Paranoia Behind Bars

How can I run like a racehorse when I'm surrounded by donkeys?

Just a week after the urine tests cleared me, the Governor called me in for a meeting. "You have the opportunity to move back into a cottage," she announced. There are only two vacancies available. "You can bring either Ahmed or Alex back with you or choose someone else." I paused, weighing my options carefully. "I think Ahmed and Alex should stay together; I'd prefer to take Meeso with me." The Governor nodded in agreement and mentioned I'd be moving into Calder C with a man named Anthony. She noted that I had developed a rapport with him and that my presence could help stabilize him—he was reportedly fragile and paranoid.

As I prepared to transition back into a cottage, I felt a sense of relief wash over me. Having been through the turmoil of the drug incident in Calder B, this opportunity was a chance to reclaim some semblance of stability. Meeso was equally excited to escape the chaos of the larger unit, while Ahmed and Alex were content to remain in Cambridge until their turn came.

However, the drama surrounding the drug find had illuminated a harsh reality: paranoia is a currency in prison. I quickly learned that trust was nearly nonexistent, and that was particularly evident in the dynamics of the inmates around me. Just days into my stay at Calder C, an incident erupted that would send shockwaves through the prison. Ahmed, one of the Muslim brothers, had a dispute with the Asian gang. The confrontation escalated quickly, and before anyone could react, Ahmed was stabbed in the neck. A Code Blue was called, and the entire prison went into lockdown for the rest of the day as investigations commenced. But as always, nobody saw anything. This incident heightened the tension in the MRC, and everyone was on high alert, especially between the Muslim crew and the Asians. Trust was shattered, and the atmosphere was thick with uncertainty as inmates speculated about reprisals.

Given that I had developed a rapport with the Muslim brotherhood, I was extra cautious now. The following days saw several acts of retaliation, and again, nobody saw anything. The whispers of violence hung in the air, and I could feel the palpable tension simmering beneath the surface. It was during this volatile week that I first encountered Farouk, a younger Muslim brother in his early 20s. Initially, he seemed like the model prisoner—calm and composed—but I soon learned he was in on a murder-related charge, allegedly acting as a getaway driver in the murder of an underworld figure named Victor P. While I didn't know much more than that at this early stage, Farouk's demeanour suggested he wasn't deeply involved in any terrorism-related activities, at least not yet.

As I settled into Calder C, I observed the dynamics of the cottage. The reality of prison life became increasingly evident; the constant undercurrent of fear and mistrust was suffocating. I kept my eyes open, aware of the shifting alliances and the potential for violence that could erupt at any moment. The horror of Ahmed's stabbing was still fresh in my mind, a stark reminder that life in prison was a deadly game where one misstep could lead to catastrophe.

I quickly became aware of the treachery that permeated the prison system. Inmates, especially those lacking social skills, often believed the worst about one another. I was determined to keep my head down and avoid becoming a target for gossip or suspicion. I maintained my walking routine with Meeso, a strategy that allowed me to escape the constant chatter and avoid the petty politics of prison life. The idea was simple: if I kept my distance from the drama, I would reduce the risk of becoming entangled in it.

But paranoia often breeds irrational behaviour. Anthony's jealousy over my rapport with the officers began to surface, and I sensed a shift in his demeanour. He began to engage in subtle intimidation, making comments loud enough for me to hear, trying to assert dominance. I recognized the signs; he was attempting to undermine my credibility and establish himself as the alpha in our shared space.

The whispers and rumours began to swirl around me, suggestions that I was an undercover operative or a snitch. The absurdity of it all was not lost on me, but in this environment, the truth often took a backseat to perception. I had to tread carefully, knowing that one wrong move could lead to deadly consequences. My sense of paranoia heightened when I overheard discussions about loyalty and betrayal. I realized that in this world, allegiances could shift in an instant, and I needed to keep my enemies close. It was a dangerous game, and I had to be vigilant at all times.

Then, a series of events unfolded that would change everything. Anthony approached me with a proposition that made my skin crawl. He wanted me to contact a man in Queensland and extort $500,000 from him. "Tell him that if he doesn't want me talking to the cops about the Harris-Scarfe scam, he should deposit the money into my account," he instructed, handing me the man's mobile phone number.

I was horrified. "No way," I replied. I had no intention of being embroiled in a scheme that could not only jeopardize my freedom but also expose my true identity. I had enough on my plate without adding extortion to the list. I tried to deflect his pressure, insisting I would be out of jail soon, never imagining I would be drawn deeper into the treachery of prison life.

Despite my reluctance, Anthony's desperation became palpable. He was not only unstable but also increasingly paranoid, fearing his own past would catch up with him. I had no intention of becoming an accomplice to his schemes, but I also knew that his paranoia could turn dangerous.

As I continued to navigate my environment, the walls of the MRC felt increasingly suffocating. I needed to keep my focus sharp, especially as I dealt with the chaos surrounding me. I had hoped to leave the turmoil behind, but with Anthony lurking in the shadows, I felt the pressure mounting. In the days leading up to a critical juncture in my mission, Anthony's behaviour grew more erratic. He often spoke about marrying Mazz, his newfound love, despite having brutally murdered his prior partner just months earlier. The absurdity of his situation was staggering, and I struggled to maintain my composure around him. When he asked me to be his best man, I snapped. "That's ridiculous, Anthony. You think a judge is going to look favourably on you marrying someone while you're awaiting trial for murder?"

His anger was palpable, but I stood firm. I refused to let his delusions draw me into a web of complicity. I was beginning to realize that Anthony was not just manipulative; he was a dangerous individual whose erratic behaviour could put my life—and my mission—at risk.

After a tumultuous few weeks, I finally received the news I had been dreading. I was called to the Central Movement Control (CMC) area one morning, where I was greeted with handcuffs and the grim realization that something was terribly wrong. The officers processed me with a cold efficiency, and I felt the weight of the unknown pressing down on me.

As I sat there, the reality of my situation sank in. Based on all the paranoia and treachery I had encountered, I knew that I was in a precarious position. The officers were watching me closely, and I had to be careful about every word I spoke and every action I took. I was determined to keep my head low and avoid the pitfalls that could lead to my downfall.

In the midst of this chaos, I continued to write letters to my family and friends, maintaining a thread of connection to the outside world. I had to keep my spirits up and remind myself of my purpose. I was there for a reason, and I couldn't let the inmates' paranoia overshadow my mission.

As the days turned into weeks, I reminded myself that survival in this environment was a daily battle. I had to keep my enemies closer while carefully navigating the treachery that surrounded me. The stakes were high, but I was determined to emerge from this ordeal unscathed, ready to reclaim my life and fulfill my duty.

Chapter 6 - Trust and Treachery: The Unwritten Rule

A man without self-control is as defenceless as a city with broken-down walls.

About a week after the urine tests cleared me, the Governor called me in for a meeting. "You have the opportunity to move back into a cottage," she announced. There are only two vacancies available. "You can bring either Ahmed or Alex back with you or choose someone else." I paused, weighing my options carefully. "I think Ahmed and Alex should stay together; I'd prefer to take Meeso with me." The Governor nodded in agreement and mentioned I'd be moving into Calder C with a man named Anthony. She noted that I had developed a rapport with him and that my presence could help stabilize him—he was reportedly fragile and paranoid.

As I prepared to transition back into a cottage, I felt a sense of relief wash over me. Having been through the turmoil of the drug incident in Calder B, this opportunity was a chance to reclaim some semblance of stability. Meeso was equally excited to escape the chaos of the larger unit, while Ahmed and Alex were content to remain in Cambridge until their turn came.

However, the drama surrounding the drug find had illuminated a harsh reality: paranoia is a currency in prison. I quickly learned that trust was nearly nonexistent, and that was particularly evident in the dynamics of the inmates around me. Just days into my stay at Calder C, an incident erupted that would send shockwaves through the prison. Ahmed, one of the Muslim brothers, had a dispute with the Asian gang. The confrontation escalated quickly, and before anyone could react, Ahmed was stabbed in the neck. A Code Blue was called, and the entire prison went into lockdown for the rest of the day as investigations commenced. But as always, nobody saw anything. This incident heightened the tension in the MRC, and everyone was on high alert, especially between the Muslim crew and the Asians. Trust was shattered, and the atmosphere was thick with uncertainty as inmates speculated about reprisals.

Given that I had developed a rapport with the Muslim brotherhood, I was extra cautious now. The following days saw several acts of retaliation, and again, nobody saw anything. The whispers of violence hung in the air, and I could feel the palpable tension simmering beneath the surface.

It was during this volatile week that I first encountered Farouk, a younger Muslim brother in his early 20s. Initially, he seemed like the model prisoner—calm and composed—but I soon learned he was in on a murder-related charge, allegedly acting as a getaway driver in the murder of an underworld figure named Victor P. While I didn't know much more than that at this early stage, Farouk's demeanor suggested he wasn't deeply involved in any terrorism-related activities, at least not yet.

As I settled into Calder C, I observed the dynamics of the cottage. The reality of prison life became increasingly evident; the constant undercurrent of fear and mistrust was suffocating. I kept my eyes open, aware of the shifting alliances and the potential for violence that could erupt at any moment. The horror of Ahmed's stabbing was still fresh in my mind, a stark reminder that life in prison was a deadly game where one misstep could lead to catastrophe.

I quickly became aware of the treachery that permeated the prison system. Inmates, especially those lacking social skills, often believed the worst about one another. I was determined to keep my head down and avoid becoming a target for gossip or suspicion. I maintained my walking routine with Meeso, a strategy that allowed me to escape the constant chatter and avoid the petty politics of prison life. The idea was simple: if I kept my distance from the drama, I would reduce the risk of becoming entangled in it.

But paranoia often breeds irrational behaviour. Anthony's jealousy over my rapport with the officers began to surface, and I sensed a shift in his demeanor. He began to engage in subtle intimidation, making comments loud enough for me to hear, trying to assert dominance. I recognized the signs; he was attempting to undermine my credibility and establish himself as the alpha in our shared space.

The whispers and rumors began to swirl around me, suggestions that I was an undercover operative or a snitch. The absurdity of it all was not lost on me, but in this environment, the truth often took a backseat to perception. I had to tread carefully, knowing that one wrong move could lead to deadly consequences.

My sense of paranoia heightened when I overheard discussions about loyalty and betrayal. I realized that in this world, allegiances could shift in an instant, and I needed to keep my enemies close. It was a dangerous game, and I had to be vigilant at all times.

Then, a series of events unfolded that would change everything. Anthony approached me with a proposition that made my skin crawl. He wanted me to contact a man in Queensland and extort $500,000 from him. "Tell him that if he doesn't want me talking to the cops about the Harris-Scarfe scam, he should deposit the money into my account," he instructed, handing me the man's mobile phone number.

I was horrified. "No way," I replied. I had no intention of being embroiled in a scheme that could not only jeopardize my freedom but also expose my true identity. I had enough on my plate without adding extortion to the list. I tried to deflect his pressure, insisting I would be out of jail soon, never imagining I would be drawn deeper into the treachery of prison life.

Despite my reluctance, Anthony's desperation became palpable. He was not only unstable but also increasingly paranoid, fearing his own past would catch up with him. I had no intention of becoming an accomplice to his schemes, but I also knew that his paranoia could turn dangerous.

As I continued to navigate my environment, the walls of the MRC felt increasingly suffocating. I needed to keep my focus sharp, especially as I dealt with the chaos surrounding me. I had hoped to leave the turmoil behind, but with Anthony lurking in the shadows, I felt the pressure mounting.

In the days leading up to a critical juncture in my mission, Anthony's behaviour grew more erratic. He often spoke about marrying Mazz, his newfound love, despite having brutally murdered his prior partner just months earlier.

The absurdity of his situation was staggering, and I struggled to maintain my composure around him. When he asked me to be his best man, I snapped. "That's ridiculous, Anthony. You think a judge is going to look favorably on you marrying someone while you're awaiting trial for murder?"

His anger was palpable, but I stood firm. I refused to let his delusions draw me into a web of complicity. I was beginning to realize that Anthony was not just manipulative; he was a dangerous individual whose erratic behaviour could put my life—and my mission—at risk.

After a tumultuous few weeks, I finally received the news I had been dreading. I was called to the Central Movement Control (CMC) area one morning, where I was greeted with handcuffs and the grim realization that something was terribly wrong. The officers processed me with a cold efficiency, and I felt the weight of the unknown pressing down on me.

As I sat there, the reality of my situation sank in. Based on all the paranoia and treachery I had encountered, I knew that I was in a precarious position. The officers were watching me closely, and I had to be careful about every word I spoke and every action I took. I was determined to keep my head low and avoid the pitfalls that could lead to my downfall.

In the midst of this chaos, I continued to write letters to my family and friends, maintaining a thread of connection to the outside world. I had to keep my spirits up and remind myself of my purpose. I was there for a reason, and I couldn't let the inmates' paranoia overshadow my mission.

As the days turned into weeks, I reminded myself that survival in this environment was a daily battle. I had to keep my enemies closer while carefully navigating the treachery that surrounded me. The stakes were high, but I was determined to emerge from this ordeal unscathed, ready to reclaim my life and fulfill my duty.

Chapter 7 - Charlotte & The Spine: Allies or Adversaries?

It's exhausting to be unforgiving. It's exhausting to be bitter. Let it go. Un-forgiveness is a "robber, a cheater of your soul." Un-forgiveness blinds us to the good in our lives; you don't see all the good things your kids are doing because you're too busy being bitter and unforgiving.

A week after the urine tests cleared me, the Governor summoned me. "You have the chance to move back into a cottage," she said, but only two vacancies were available. "You can bring either Ahmed or Alex back with you, or choose someone else." I quickly responded, "I think Ahmed and Alex should stay together; I'd rather take Meeso with me." The Governor agreed, also suggesting I move in with a guy named Anthony. She noted my rapport with him and mentioned that he was fragile and paranoid, believing my presence would help stabilize him.

As I transitioned back into a cottage, I felt a surge of relief. After the chaotic events surrounding the drug incident in Calder B, this opportunity felt like a chance to reclaim some stability. Meeso was equally thrilled to escape the larger unit, while Ahmed and Alex were content to remain in Cambridge until their turn came.

However, the recent turmoil had shed light on a darker reality: paranoia ruled this environment. I quickly realized that trust was a rare commodity in prison. In my new home, I kept a close watch on Anthony, aware of the potential threats he posed—not just to my safety, but to my undercover mission as well.

It wasn't long before the Homicide Squad approached me with a request that could change the course of my mission. They wanted my assistance in gathering intel on Anthony. His plan to claim mental impairment during his trial for the brutal murder of his partner could derail the case against him. They needed me to extract as much information as I could from him—evidence that could solidify the charges and ensure he faced justice. I was happy to help, knowing it was my moral duty, especially for the victim's family. I understood the significance of bringing someone like Anthony to justice, and I was determined to do my part.

The atmosphere in Calder C seemed deceptively calm at first, but under the surface, tensions simmered. Just days into my stay, an incident erupted that sent shockwaves throughout the prison. Ahmed, one of the Muslim brothers, got into a heated dispute with the Asian gang. No sooner had the arguments begun than Ahmed was stabbed in the neck. A Code Blue echoed through the halls, and the entire prison went into lockdown for the rest of the day while investigations unfolded. As was the norm, nobody saw anything. The incident amplified the already fraught atmosphere, and I could feel the palpable tension between the Muslim crew and the Asians. Trust evaporated, replaced by an urgent need to assess what would happen next.

Given my rapport with the Muslim brotherhood, I was extra cautious. The following days saw several reprisals, with whispers of violence filling the air. Rumours spread like wildfire, but again, nobody saw anything. The prison was a cauldron of suspicion, and I needed to stay on high alert.

As I settled into my routine at the MRC, I observed the heightened activity among the Muslim brothers. Their discussions became increasingly animated, often planning and strategizing in hushed tones. I knew I had to navigate this landscape carefully, trying to engage with them to gather as much intelligence as possible about their activities. This heightened activity was significant; I needed to understand their motivations and any potential threats they posed.

I kept to myself, maintaining my walking routine with Meeso as a way to avoid the incessant gossip and drama that permeated prison life. My theory was simple: if I wasn't present when something went down, I wouldn't be blamed for it. Yet, the treachery in this place could ensnare anyone, regardless of their intentions.

But as I became more entrenched in this world, I realized that my seemingly settled existence in Calder C was being turned upside down. Anthony's jealousy festered, and he began to throw subtle intimidation my way, trying to assert dominance. I could sense that he was treacherous, willing to do anything to garner favor with the hardened criminals around us. It didn't take long for me to conclude that he was a jailhouse snitch, a 'dog' who would betray anyone to save his own skin.

The paranoia among the inmates was palpable. I had encountered a group of inmates in the Cambridge Unit led by Alan and Stuart, who had sensed my unease and perceived me as a threat. Their hostility manifested in barbed comments aimed at undermining my credibility. Ignoring their taunts was my only option; engaging would only elevate their status and validate their insecurities.

As my time in Charlotte progressed, I was drawn deeper into the web of prison life. The whispers and rumours began to swirl around me, suggesting that I was an undercover operative or a snitch. The absurdity of it all was not lost on me, but in this environment, the truth often took a backseat to perception. I had to tread carefully, knowing that one wrong move could lead to deadly consequences.

Then, as if the universe were conspiring against me, Anthony made an allegation against me, claiming I was conspiring with the officers. I was called into the Central Movement Control area, where I was handcuffed and led into a room for questioning. The fear gripped me as I faced a panel of officials, unsure of what I had supposedly done.

I felt the walls closing in, my heart racing as I realized that Anthony's treachery had put my mission—and my life—at risk. I was now under suspicion, trapped in a web of accusations and paranoia.

While I sat in Exford, I tried to keep my mind sharp, but the isolation weighed heavily on me. I wrote letters to my family, maintaining a connection to the outside world, but I felt the stress of my situation bearing down. I knew I had to focus on my mission, gathering intelligence while keeping my true identity hidden.

As the days dragged on, the tension in the prison escalated. I continued to observe the Muslim brothers, aware that their plans could have significant ramifications. I needed to remain vigilant, always aware of my surroundings, and be ready to adapt as the situation evolved.

The prison was a cauldron of paranoia, and I had to navigate it carefully. Each day was a battle for survival, both physically and mentally. I was determined not to let Anthony's betrayal define me. Instead, I would use it as fuel to drive my mission forward, ensuring that I would emerge from this ordeal stronger and more resilient.

Through the chaos, I reminded myself that I was there for a reason. I needed to gather information, understand the dynamics at play, and ultimately fulfill my duty. I would continue to forge ahead, focused on my goals, determined to navigate the treacherous waters of prison life while keeping my enemies closer.

Chapter 8 - Secrets of the Cell: What Stays Behind Bars

We can forgive a child for being afraid of the dark, but the real tragedy in life is when men are afraid of the light!

While nestled in the confines of Charlotte, often referred to as the "Slot," I received a message from my handlers. They notified me that Anthony had somehow managed to contact my family on the outside. The implications were chilling; he had crossed a line that should never have been breached. The betrayal stung, and I felt a surge of anger. Anthony's actions were a direct violation of the unspoken rule that you never involve anyone outside prison walls in your internal affairs.

Living in the Slot was a test of endurance. Each inmate was granted a mere two hours a day in an exercise yard that measured about five meters by seven meters. During that time, I often found myself alone, pacing the perimeter with nothing but my thoughts. The rest of my day was marked by 22 hours of lockdown in a cramped cell, a dismal space measuring just two meters wide by four meters long. Inside, I had a very skinny single bed with a thin 4-inch foam mattress, a toilet without a seat—because the seats are considered a weapon—a small wash basin, and a cramped shower. A tiny window offered a bleak view of concrete walls and razor wire, the light filtering through only to illuminate the despair that surrounded me. The silence was deafening, amplifying the feelings of isolation and helplessness that seeped into my bones. With no indication of how long I would be kept there, I felt the walls closing in, a constant reminder of my precarious situation.

Despite the overwhelming sense of helplessness, I made a conscious decision to keep myself active in both mind and body. I refused to let the confinement crush my spirit. I read anything I could get my hands on, devouring books that offered an escape from the grim reality of prison life. I also set a grueling routine for myself, committing to 200 push-ups and 200 sit-ups each day, along with other exercises I could manage in my confined space. Yet, despite my efforts, communication was limited, making it challenging to gather the intel I needed for my mission.

Amidst the isolation, I soon discovered that several of the Muslim brothers, those suspected of planning terrorist plots on Australian soil, were also in the Slot. This was a double-edged sword; while their presence could provide valuable insights, it also heightened the stakes. I needed to tread carefully, as my inability to deal with Anthony's betrayal weighed heavily on my conscience.

The tension in the Slot escalated quickly. I witnessed one inmate set his mattress on fire at 2 AM, igniting chaos in the otherwise quiet hall. The flames flickered menacingly, and the smell of smoke permeated the air, stirring panic among the inmates. Guards rushed in, their shouts echoing as they ordered everyone to evacuate Charlotte temporarily. The commotion was maddening; the clatter of boots and the frantic voices blended into a cacophony of mayhem. I stood in the cold, waiting for the chaos to subside, feeling the adrenaline coursing through my veins as I took in the scene. It was a stark reminder of the volatility of prison life.

Despite the madness, I focused on my surroundings, using the opportunity to observe the reactions of the Muslim brothers as they navigated the chaos. Their body language spoke volumes; they were on high alert, whispering urgently among themselves. This was my chance to gather intel while remaining inconspicuous, but the distraction of Anthony's betrayal gnawed at me.

Days passed with a heavy silence, broken only by the muffled sounds of life outside my cell. I remained vigilant, aware that Anthony's paranoia could spiral out of control at any moment. I kept my interactions with the Muslim brothers discreet, carefully gauging their intentions and gathering insights without drawing attention to myself. Yet, the tension grew, and I could feel Anthony's resentment simmering beneath the surface.

Then, the unexpected happened. Anthony approached me with a disturbing proposition that made my stomach churn. He wanted me to contact a man in Queensland and extort $500,000 from him. "Tell him that if he doesn't want me talking to the cops about the Harris-Scarfe scam, he should deposit the money into my account," he instructed, handing me the man's mobile number.

I was horrified. "I'm not doing that," I replied firmly. The thought of being embroiled in such a scheme was not only dangerous but could also jeopardize my mission. I had enough to navigate without adding extortion to the mix. In my mind, I had no intention of becoming a pawn in Anthony's twisted game.

In the days that followed, I kept my distance from Anthony, aware of how his jealousy and paranoia could spiral dangerously. I focused on my interactions with the Muslim brothers, gathering insights while keeping my true purpose hidden. But the tension was palpable, and I knew I had to stay vigilant.

As I navigated the complexities of prison life, I continued to witness the pervasive paranoia among the inmates. There was a constant undercurrent of fear and suspicion, and I was determined not to become a target. I had to keep my enemies close while remaining focused on my mission.

One fateful night, I overheard a conversation that sent chills down my spine. The Muslim brothers were discussing plans that hinted at larger operations within the prison system. I knew I had to gather as much intel as possible while remaining inconspicuous. The stakes were high, and I was determined to ensure that my mission was successful.

Despite the chaos swirling around me, I clung to the belief that I could navigate this treacherous environment. I had to stay sharp, avoid entanglement in rumours, and focus on gathering the intel that would aid the Homicide Squad in their pursuit of justice. I reminded myself constantly that this was my duty, not just for myself, but for the victim and her family.

The days seemed to stretch into weeks, and I found myself caught in a web of tension and uncertainty. I needed to maintain my cover while gathering critical information about the Muslim brothers and the treachery surrounding Anthony. Each day was a battle for survival, but I was resolute in my determination to emerge from this ordeal unscathed and fulfill my mission.

Chapter 9 - The Prison Merry-Go-Round: No Escape

Light travels faster than sound. That's why some people appear to be bright until you hear them speak.

On April 11, 2007, I found myself grappling with the consequences of Anthony's betrayal. His decision to reach out to my family had shattered the unspoken code of prison life. I had never uttered Anthony's name to anyone, and the realization that he had made contact with my loved ones left me feeling a surge of anger and disbelief. What kind of coward writes to someone's family to stir up trouble?

In my view, the rule was clear: what happens in jail stays in jail. I had shielded my family from the turmoil of my existence in the MRC and the Slot, believing they deserved to remain insulated from the chaos that enveloped me. The moment I learned of Anthony's actions, a deep fury bubbled within me. "How did he get our address?" I thought. His childish need to provoke me was infuriating, and for a fleeting moment, I felt the urge to confront him physically.

Calming down after that realization was a challenge, but I managed to regain my composure. I had conducted myself with respect during my time at the MRC, and Anthony's actions felt like a taint on my integrity. I would not give him the satisfaction of knowing he had upset me. I would not, could not, stoop to his level.

As I continued my daily routine, I noticed the tension in the air. The Muslim brothers were becoming more vocal, and their discussions hinted at broader operations that could have serious implications. I was determined to stay engaged and gather insights into their plans while remaining inconspicuous. My interactions with them became increasingly crucial; I needed to understand their motives and potential threats.

Then, on April 29, 2007, I was abruptly called to the Central Movement Control area. Handcuffed and led into a room for questioning, I faced a panel of officials. They informed me that another prisoner had made an allegation against me, leaving me in a state of confusion and vulnerability. I felt utterly helpless as they provided no specifics, and my mind raced with possibilities. I had to tread carefully, knowing that my situation could quickly escalate into a dangerous game of survival.

Days turned into weeks, and I continued to navigate the uncertainty of my situation. The growing paranoia among the inmates weighed heavily on me, especially as the Homicide Squad's request for intel loomed in my thoughts. I was determined not to let Anthony's betrayal define my experience. Instead, I focused on my task, gathering intel on the Muslim brothers while keeping my cover intact.

The days turned into a blur of tension and uncertainty. I remained vigilant, acutely aware of the dangers lurking behind every corner. My interactions with the Muslim brothers were critical; I was committed to uncovering the truth about their plans. Every conversation could lead to vital information, and I needed to maintain my focus, knowing that the stakes were high—not just for me but for the families affected by Anthony's actions.

In the midst of this turmoil, I often reflected on my life in the Slot. The small confines of my cell—a skinny single bed, a 4-inch foam mattress, a toilet without a seat, a tiny wash basin, and a cramped shower—were stifling. The solitude was deafening, and the weight of my situation pressed down upon me. Yet, I persisted, driven by a determination to emerge from this ordeal stronger and more resilient.

As I continued to gather intelligence and navigate the complexities of prison life, I reminded myself that I was there for a reason. I would not let fear or paranoia dictate my actions. My mission was clear: to ensure that justice was served, and I would do whatever it took to achieve that goal.

Chapter 10 - Tommy C and Frankie B: The Oddities of Jail

Light travels faster than sound. That's why some people appear to be bright until you hear them speak.

On May 2, 2007, just as I had begun to settle into the uneasy rhythm of life at Bellfield unit in Ararat, I received the dreaded knock on my cell door. The officer stood there, clipboard in hand, his expression unreadable. "Pack your bags… You're on the bus!" Confusion hit me like a cold wave. I had thought I would be staying at Port Phillip for some time, but now I was being ripped away once again.

As I shuffled through the motions, a gnawing apprehension twisted in my gut. Where was I headed? It wasn't until we reached the front admissions building that I discovered the unsettling truth: I was being transferred to Ararat prison. My heart sank. I had only heard whispers about this place, and nothing good. Apprehension morphed into dread; to say I was uneasy was an understatement.

The drive to Ararat felt interminable. We were packed tightly in the cattle truck, four others in my compartment. A small window offered a glimpse of the outside world, but peering out would draw unwanted attention. I remained silent, listening to the usual banter among the others—their bravado masking the fear that simmered beneath the surface. "How long you got?" "What unit were you in?" "Ever been to Ararat before?" I kept my distance; I didn't come to jail to make friends. Their tales of bravado and past crimes washed over me like white noise, a reminder of the world I was trying to escape.

When we finally arrived at Ararat, I was greeted not by the imposing walls of a maximum-security prison but by the sight of gum trees. Yet, the natural beauty did little to soothe my nerves. Standing beside the van, officers began the familiar admission process. "Name, date of birth, CRN; OK, you can go in now." The processing was noticeably more relaxed than at MRC or Port Phillip—perhaps because it was a medium-security prison—but that didn't lessen the indignity of the urine test and strip-search. Each encounter with the officers felt like a violation, a reminder of my status as little more than a number in an unforgiving system.

We were issued our green clothing and work gear. Ararat was another working jail; there was no choice but to labor for a measly $5 a day. I was assigned to a Cleaning Billet, which gave me access to all areas, including the Officers' quarters. This job would allow me to gather valuable intel, but it also placed me in close proximity to the darker corners of prison life.

By the time I reached my new cell in Bellfield unit around 3 PM, the weight of the day pressed heavily on my shoulders. While I was relieved to be in a medium-security prison, I was still furious about being shunted to the arse-end of the world. The distance from Melbourne meant less access to visitors, my solicitor, and family. I was now facing STD rates on all my calls, and the thought of spending my limited funds on phone calls to stay connected was infuriating.

As I entered cell 10, I was immediately struck by the atmosphere. It was still a jail, but compared to the enclosed and intense environments of MRC, Port Phillip, and Charlotte, Ararat felt less suffocating. The cells were three-outers, meaning I would have two cellmates rather than one. The incumbent cellmate was a young Aboriginal guy named Bryn, who seemed relatively harmless, while the other cellmate, Rodney, arrived on the same day. He appeared timid and frightened, yet friendly enough.

Despite the three-outer situation, the cells at Ararat were recently refurbished, making them cleaner and more comfortable than the filth I had endured in Charlotte and Port Phillip. However, the presence of two other inmates meant that privacy would be a constant issue, with the toilet in full view.

In the first few days, I tried to develop a rapport with Rodney, who suited my placid nature, even if he had strange tendencies—like preferring to stay in the dark. Whenever I left the room, he would immediately turn off the lights, an odd quirk I found irritating. Bryn, on the other hand, was a classic bullshit artist, claiming to be a former basketball superstar who had received a scholarship from UCLA. My background in the sport made it hard for me to take him seriously; jails were full of exaggerations and bravado.

Tension lingered in the air as I settled into my new life. I soon learned that Ararat was a haven for the worst of the worst—long-serving pedophiles and those convicted of heinous crimes. The thought of sharing space with such individuals weighed heavily on my mind. The reality of my surroundings began to sink in, and I was constantly reminded of the treachery that could lurk behind any corner.

Then, the violence began to surface. One day, I witnessed an inmate in the factory where they made number plates being attacked by four others, a brutal display of betrayal that left me shaken. The chaos erupted without warning, and the sounds of fists meeting flesh echoed in my ears.

In a place like this, loyalties shifted like sand, and the threat of violence was always looming.

I couldn't ignore the underlying currents of danger. The constant threat of physical harm was a stark reminder that in this world, trust was a luxury I could not afford. While I worked diligently to gather intel, I had to keep my guard up, aware that one misstep could lead to dire consequences.

As days turned into a blur of tension and uncertainty, I remained focused on my mission. I needed to navigate the complexities of prison life while staying vigilant against the looming threats that surrounded me. The stakes were high, not just for me, but for the families affected by the treachery and violence that permeated this place.

My resolve hardened as I reminded myself that I was there for a reason. I had to ensure that justice would be served, and I would do whatever it took to achieve that goal. In the shadows of Ararat, I would not let fear dictate my actions. The game was dangerous, but I was determined to play it to the end.

Chapter 11 - Road Trips Through Confinement

I demolish my bridges behind me... then there is no choice but to move forward.

In the days that followed, I quickly realized just how peculiar my new cellmate, Tom, truly was. His unsettling habits were more than just quirks; they were a red flag in a world where danger lurked around every corner. The most alarming of these was his refusal to wash or shower. After three or four days of enduring his stench, I could no longer hold my tongue. "Tom, you really should shower and change your clothes," I suggested, trying to mask my disgust.

He shrugged it off, a vacant look in his eyes. "Nah, I'm okay. I don't need to shower because I'm a naturally clean person. I haven't used toilet paper in 15 years; I just wash with water." Rodney and I exchanged incredulous glances, unable to suppress our laughter at his bizarre logic. But the humour faded quickly, overshadowed by the dread of sharing a cell with someone so unhinged.

As I settled into my new life in Ararat, I was acutely aware of the heightened activity among the Muslim brothers, particularly a faction that called themselves the "Prisoners of God." Their influence was palpable, and when they decided I had to go, they made my life increasingly unbearable. They began to isolate me, using a mix of intimidation and psychological warfare. It started with hushed whispers and pointed glares whenever I entered a room.

One night, as I returned from a shift in the factory, I found my cell ransacked. My personal items were strewn across the floor, a clear message that I was no longer welcome. The bullying escalated; they would block my path in the corridors, taunting me with veiled threats. "You should watch your back, mate," one of them sneered, his eyes glinting with malice. They even went so far as to knock on my cell door late at night, shouting slurs and insults designed to provoke fear.

Then came the physical intimidation. One day, I was cornered in the yard by three of the "Prisoners of God," who started pushing me around, shoving me against the wall. "You think you can just walk in here and gather intel?" one growled, his face inches from mine. My heart raced, and I fought to keep my composure. "I'm just doing my time," I replied, trying to sound calm, but I could feel the sweat beading on my forehead.

In the midst of this turmoil, I found an unexpected ally in another Muslim brother, a Turk named Kabil B. He was an interesting character, fiercely independent and not part of the "Prisoners of God." Kabil quickly developed a trust and liking for me, and his presence proved to be a lifeline during this tumultuous time. He had his enemies, but he could handle himself well in a fight. "You're alright, mate," he said one day, nodding as we exchanged information about the prison dynamics. "Just keep your head down and let me know if those idiots give you trouble."

Kabil's alliance was invaluable. He had a way of maneuvering through the prison's social structure that I didn't yet fully understand. His insights into the inner workings of the Muslim brothers provided me with the intelligence I desperately needed. It was a delicate balance, though; I had to navigate my interactions with Kabil while remaining cautious of the "Prisoners of God."

One fateful night, after a particularly tense day where I had received more threats, I overheard whispers about a significant operation being planned by the Muslim brothers. The details were sparse, but I sensed the urgency behind their discussions. Gathering this intel became my priority, but I felt the weight of their scrutiny; their gazes were sharp, and the tension in the air was thick enough to cut with a knife.

The atmosphere was suffocating, and anxiety clawed at my insides, leaving me in a state of vulnerability. My mind raced as I tried to decipher the motives behind this betrayal. Was it a distraction orchestrated by Anthony, or had the "Prisoners of God" finally figured me out? My gut told me it was Anthony—he had realized I knew too much.

Days turned into weeks, and I continued to navigate the uncertainty of my situation. The Homicide Squad's request for intel weighed heavily on my conscience as I attempted to gather information on the Muslim brothers while remaining inconspicuous. The stakes were higher than ever; I was surrounded by dangerous individuals, and every interaction could lead to peril.

As I settled into the daily grind, I kept my focus on my mission. I had to balance the need for information with the ever-present danger of exposure. Every conversation could yield valuable insights, but I had to be careful—I was walking a tightrope, and one misstep could mean the difference between life and death.

In the midst of the chaos, I reminded myself that I was there for a reason. I had a mission to complete, and I would not allow Anthony's treachery to derail my purpose. The days seemed to stretch into weeks, but I remained vigilant, determined to gather the intel necessary to aid the Homicide Squad in their pursuit of justice. With allies like Kabil and the ever-present threat of the "Prisoners of God," I steeled myself for the challenges ahead, knowing that survival in this unforgiving world depended on my ability to adapt and endure.

Chapter 12 - Drugs, Medication, and Control in the Jail System

We don't live in a world of reality; we live in a world of perceptions.

As I settled into my time at Ararat, I quickly became aware of the pervasive prescription drug use infiltrating the prison system. The extent of medication reliance was shocking; a staggering 75% of inmates in my unit were on some form of medication at least once a day. Pill dispensing occurred three times daily—morning, afternoon, and evening—and it was evident that many men were accessing their meds regularly. This rampant reliance on pharmaceuticals was a management tool for the prison system, keeping inmates calmer and easier to control.

However, this easy access to medication also fostered a thriving black market for trafficking and trading drugs. While officers enforced strict protocols requiring inmates to swallow their pills under watchful eyes, many quickly learned how to hide their medications, regurgitating them in the privacy of their cells. The desperation for drugs created a chaotic environment where inmates willingly shared pills that had already been in someone else's mouth, unaware of the potential consequences.

One inmate, Michael N—a Canadian in his late 50s and a known HIV-AIDS carrier—was notorious for trading his pills. He'd swallow them in front of the officers only to spit them out later for eager buyers. The risks involved were astounding, yet many inmates participated, willing to gamble their health for a brief escape from their grim reality.

In the midst of this chaos, I found myself grappling with the growing threat of violence that loomed over me. The "Prisoners of God" crew had marked me as a target, and I needed to tread carefully. One evening, a young thug named James H confronted me. Known for beating an old grandfather to a pulp with a wooden weapon, he was a violent white supremacist trying to gain acceptance within his gang. I could see the hunger for respect in his eyes as he approached me, his intentions clear.

"Listen, you're fucken dead, cunt," he snarled, locking the door behind him. My heart raced as I recognized the gravity of the situation. James was younger, fit, and clearly looking to assert his dominance. I knew all too well the prison code: if you let them beat you, you were done. I was not going to be a victim.

"Only one of us will walk out of here alive," I replied, my voice steady despite the adrenaline coursing through me. The next five to six minutes felt like an eternity as we clashed in a brutal struggle, each of us fighting for survival. The room echoed with the sounds of our bodies colliding, fists meeting flesh, and the air grew thick with tension.

When it was over, I stood over James, panting heavily. He lay on the ground, his arms broken, a shattered leg, and a face that was unrecognizable, needing 90 stitches. I later learned he had suffered a ruptured lung as well. I didn't know what had come over me; nobody truly knows how they will react until their life is threatened. I refused to let this despicable piece of shit defeat me, nor would I allow the "Prisoners of God" crew to claim victory.

After I walked out of that room, James was discovered sometime later by another inmate, but the story was shrouded in silence. Nobody saw anything, or if they did, they weren't talking. I had cleaned myself up before leaving the cell, and while everyone knew something had happened, nobody truly knew. This was jail, after all. I faced multiple interrogations from the officers, but their indifference made it clear they didn't care about James; in fact, I got the impression they relished in his demise, especially considering his cowardly act of bashing an old pensioner.

The aftermath of the fight brought a newfound respect from some inmates, but I was also acutely aware of the lingering threat from the "Prisoners of God." Would they come after me again? This uncertainty added another layer of stress to my already complicated mission, creating a nightmare that distracted me from my objectives.

Despite the chaos surrounding me, I remained focused on the intel I had gathered regarding the Muslim brothers and their potential plans for a terrorist attack at the MCG. The urgency to relay this information to my handlers weighed heavily on my conscience, and I was determined to ensure the threat was taken seriously.

I observed how drugs could easily enter the system through visits; often, a visitor would swallow them and transfer them during a kiss. The lengths some individuals went to for drugs were astonishing, and I witnessed inmates devising elaborate schemes to smuggle drugs into the prison. It was clear the drug culture was deeply entrenched within Ararat's walls.

As I continued my undercover mission, I remained focused on gathering information about the Muslim brothers while keeping an eye on the growing drug trade around me. The tension in the unit was palpable, and I navigated my interactions carefully, knowing that one slip could jeopardize my mission.

In the following days, I was extracted multiple times under the guise of needing urgent medical attention. This allowed me to meet with my handlers discreetly and provide updates on the intel I had gathered, particularly regarding the potential attack at the MCG and Abdul BN's involvement. Each extraction was a carefully orchestrated opportunity to ensure that my findings did not go unnoticed.

While the chaos of prison life continued to swirl around me, I remained resolute in my mission. The information I had about the Muslim brothers was critical, and I was determined to relay it effectively to my handlers. The stakes were high, and I knew that every moment counted. As the days passed, I pressed on, navigating the complexities of prison life while gathering the intel necessary to aid the Homicide Squad in their pursuit of justice. The urgency of my mission fueled my determination, and I was committed to ensuring that the information I had reached the right people before it was too late.

Chapter 13 - The Phantom Shitter: Tales of the Unseen

We do not inherit the earth from our ancestors. We have borrowed it from our children.

As I settled into life in the Unit at Ararat, I quickly came to realize just how peculiar my cellmate, Tom, really was. His bizarre habits were alarming, especially his outright refusal to wash or shower. After enduring his odour for a few days, I finally confronted him. "Tom, you really need to clean up," I urged, hoping to appeal to some sense of hygiene.

He shrugged it off, a glazed look in his eyes. "Nah, I'm fine. I don't need to shower because I'm a naturally clean person. I haven't used toilet paper in 15 years; I just wash with water." Rodney and I exchanged incredulous glances, struggling to suppress our laughter at his warped logic. But the humour faded quickly when I remembered my real mission: gathering intel on the Muslim brothers and their activities.

Tension in the unit escalated after my confrontation with James H. The "Prisoners of God" crew had marked me, and their eyes were ever-watchful. I could feel the hostility brewing, and every corner I turned felt like a potential ambush. I was starting to get the sense that James's defeat hadn't silenced the gang; it had only intensified their desire to assert dominance over me.

One evening, as I lay in bed, the muffled sounds of laughter and shouting echoed through the unit. I peered out of my cell and saw a group of inmates gathered in the common area, their faces twisted in excitement as they cheered on a fight, the brutal spectacle drawing them in like moths to a flame. I felt a knot tighten in my stomach; the violence was a constant reminder that I was living in a powder keg, and any spark could ignite chaos.

Days passed, and I found myself increasingly on edge. The threats from the "Prisoners of God" were palpable, and I knew they were looking for an opportunity to retaliate. One night, I overheard whispers about a planned attack on me, their voices laced with venom. "He thinks he can take on James and walk away unscathed," one sneered, his tone dripping with contempt. I knew I had to be prepared for whatever they had in store.

Amidst this turmoil, I continued to gather intel on the Muslim brothers. One fateful night, I overheard discussions about a potential terrorist attack at the MCG in Melbourne. My heart raced as I realized the implications of the intel I had stumbled upon. The name Abdul BN came up frequently, and it was clear he was heavily involved in the planning. I knew I had to gather as much detailed information as possible and find a way to relay it to my handlers without raising suspicion.

But the challenges of relaying this crucial intel weighed heavily on me. The prison environment was fraught with tension and paranoia, and I had to be strategic in how I communicated with my handlers. Fortunately, the Homicide Squad's interest in Anthony D provided a convenient cover, allowing me to be extracted under the guise of needing urgent medical attention.

One particularly tense evening, I witnessed Tom in a daze, sitting on the toilet with blood pooling around him. Panic surged through me as I cautiously approached him, trying to assess the situation without alarming him. "Tom, are you okay?" I whispered, but when he didn't respond, I felt the clock ticking. I had to act quickly to avoid drawing the attention of the officers.

In that moment, I remembered my primary mission. I coaxed Tom into the shower to clean himself up, maintaining my composure as I cleaned up the blood. It was a tense moment, and I knew that if the officers found out, it could lead to serious consequences for both of us. After ensuring Tom was stable, I felt a surge of relief wash over me, but I also knew that I couldn't let my guard down; the stakes were too high.

As the days turned into a blur of tension and urgency, I grew increasingly aware of my surroundings. The "Prisoners of God" crew continued to challenge me, and I found myself in more precarious situations. One afternoon, I was cornered in the yard by a group of them, their hostile glares cutting through me like daggers. "You think you can just stroll around here after taking out James?" one of them growled, flexing his muscles as he stepped closer.

"Maybe you should learn your place, mate," I replied, feigning confidence. The moment felt charged; I was aware that showing fear could lead to dire consequences. But I was also acutely aware of Kabil's presence nearby. He stepped forward, his eyes hardening as he positioned himself beside me. "You want to take this further?" he challenged, his voice low and menacing. The tension hung thick in the air, but the "Prisoners of God" retreated, recognizing that they were outnumbered for the moment.

Kabil proved to be an invaluable ally. He had his own enemies but carried a formidable reputation that commanded respect. His insights into the prison dynamics provided me with the intelligence I needed, and his friendship offered a glimmer of hope amid the chaos. As we shared stories of our pasts, I felt a bond forming; we were both trapped in this hellish environment, fighting to survive.

In the following days, I continued to navigate the complexities of prison life while gathering the intel necessary to aid the Homicide Squad in their pursuit of justice. Each day became a delicate balancing act, fraught with the ever-present danger of exposure. I was determined to ensure that the information I had about the potential attack reached the right people before it was too late.

As the stakes rose, I remained resolute in my mission, knowing that the information I possessed could save lives. I pressed on, aware that each moment counted, and I was committed to uncovering the truth about the Muslim brothers and their plans. In the shadows of Ararat, I steeled myself for the challenges ahead, knowing that survival depended on my ability to adapt and endure.

Chapter 14 - Whispers of Danger: Gathering Intel

I demolish my bridges behind me… then there is no choice but to move forward.

If this all sounds a little disjointed, it's because it is. That's precisely the nature of jail; the prison guards try to keep you as ill-informed and as wrong-footed as possible. The frustration of this environment gnawed at me, so I often found solace in writing poems and letters for other inmates. A few blokes at Ararat asked me to pen verses for their girlfriends or wives, and I obliged. It became a form of therapy for me, a fleeting escape from the absurdity of prison life that surrounded me.

One day, while chatting with a guy nicknamed "Noodles," who was harmless but clearly fried from drugs, I asked about his girlfriend. "We met at the Ferntree Gully Boarding House," he said, his eyes glassy. I thought, "I can work with that." But when I asked if she had a nickname, he replied, "She's kind of cuddly." At that point, I knew he meant she was a bush-pig, and I couldn't help but laugh, if only briefly. Humour felt like a luxury in this place.

Yet, amid these lighter moments, the gravity of my undercover mission weighed heavily on my shoulders. I was gathering intel on the Muslim brothers, and the stakes could not have been higher. I recently stumbled upon alarming information about a possible terrorist attack at the MCG. The name Abdul NB surfaced repeatedly in hushed conversations, and I knew I needed to document every detail I could gather. The challenge lay in figuring out how to relay this information to my handlers without raising the suspicions of the other inmates.

As I settled into a routine in Sirius Unit, I encountered Tom, my cellmate, whose peculiar habits were hard to ignore. He rarely washed or changed his clothes, and after a few days of enduring his stench, I finally suggested he take a shower. His response left both Rodney and me in stitches, but the humour faded quickly when I realized the urgency of my mission overshadowed our odd interactions.

Then, on the fifth night, I woke up to find Tom sitting on the toilet in a daze, blood trickling down his leg. Panic surged through me as I assessed the situation. I had to act quickly to avoid alerting the officers. "Tom, are you okay?" I whispered, but he stared blankly ahead, lost in his own world. I coaxed him into the shower, cleaned up the blood, and made him swear to keep the incident a secret. My focus remained unwavering: I had to gather intel on the Muslim brothers and ensure that information about the potential attack reached my handlers.

Days turned into a blur of tension and urgency as the atmosphere in the unit soured. The "Prisoners of God" crew was relentless, and the whispers of danger heightened my anxiety. They were prowling around, watching me, and I could sense the hostility brewing beneath the surface. One day, I overheard a couple of them plotting and laughing sinisterly in the corner. "He thinks he can take on James and walk away unscathed," one of them sneered, sending chills down my spine.

Then there was Frank B, a despicable piece of work serving time for horrific animal cruelty. He had a reputation for doing unspeakable things—digging holes for cats or dogs, placing them in the ground, and then running over them with a lawnmower. I couldn't stand the sight of him, and the thought of what he had done made my skin crawl.

One afternoon, as he emerged from the shower, I took my chance. I locked the door behind me, my heart pounding in my chest. "You think you can just walk around here like you own the place?" I growled, a surge of adrenaline coursing through me. Before he could react, I lunged at him, beating him senseless. It wasn't as brutal as my encounter with James, but I left him with two broken arms and a few other injuries that would take weeks to heal.

Afterward, I sat in my cell, haunted by what I had done. I wasn't proud of myself, and I couldn't shake the unsettling feeling that had settled in my stomach. How had jail changed me? The realization weighed heavily on my conscience as I contemplated the man I was becoming. I knew that nobody had seen or heard anything, but the act itself gnawed at me in the dark hours of the night.

In the midst of this chaos, I received a message from the Homicide Squad. They arranged for me to be extracted several times over the next few days under the pretense of needing urgent medical attention. Each extraction felt like a double-edged sword; while it allowed my handlers to meet with me discreetly, it also heightened the tension among the inmates. I could almost feel the eyes of the "Prisoners of God" crew boring into me, their whispers growing louder.

Every time I was extracted, I felt a mix of urgency and anxiety—this was my chance to relay information that could prevent a tragedy. But the fear of being discovered gnawed at me. Would they notice the change in my demeanor? Would they put two and two together and realize I was the one gathering intel?

The pressure continued to mount as I navigated my interactions with the Muslim brothers, who were becoming increasingly vocal about their plans. I had to remain vigilant, balancing the need to engage with them while keeping my cover intact. Each conversation became a high-stakes game, and I was determined to ensure that the intel I gathered about the MCG threat, particularly involving Abdul BN, was communicated effectively.

As the days passed, I pressed on, navigating the complexities of prison life while gathering the intel necessary to aid the Homicide Squad in their pursuit of justice. The danger was palpable, and I felt the weight of responsibility on my shoulders. With the looming threat of the "Prisoners of God" crew and the growing tensions among the Muslim brothers, I knew I was walking a tightrope—and one misstep could lead to disaster.

In the shadows of Ararat, I steeled myself for the challenges ahead, knowing that survival depended on my ability to adapt and endure. Each day brought new challenges, but I was resolute in my mission. I would ensure that my handlers received the information they needed to act swiftly and decisively before it was too late.

Chapter 15 - The Final Road Trip: The Betrayal Lingers

"Betrayal is never easy to handle, but it is a lesson in trust." – Unknown

The day I was loaded onto the van with four other blokes, a sense of dread washed over me. Three of us were headed to Langi Kal Kal, while two were on their way to Ararat. Among my companions was John B, someone I recognized from my MRC days, but the others were strangers. The uncertainty of the move weighed heavily on my mind. I felt the familiar pang of anxiety—this was a tactic of the corrections system, designed to keep us unsettled and off-balance. I had to maintain my focus on gathering intel on the Muslim brothers while bracing myself for the unknown of the next prison.

As the van jolted along the road, my thoughts spiraled. Would Langi Kal Kal offer a reprieve from the chaos of Ararat, or would it plunge me into another nightmare? The van had a decent-sized window, and I took in the passing countryside, a stark reminder of the freedom I had lost. Most of the time I'd spent in a van over the past 18 months felt like a blur, and now, seeing the outside world ignited a flicker of longing within me. It's amazing what we take for granted when our lives are reduced to concrete walls and iron bars.

Upon arriving at Langi Kal Kal (LKK), located about 43 kilometers past Ballarat in Trawalla, I felt a mix of relief and apprehension. I had heard whispers about LKK being an open camp, a significant improvement after the claustrophobic confines of Port Phillip and Ararat. I was determined to keep myself busy and out of jail politics as much as possible.

One of the first things I noticed was the expansive grounds; LKK sprawled over 2,900 acres, offering plenty of room to breathe. There was a 6–7 km bushwalking track that became my sanctuary. After being restricted to an exercise yard no bigger than a small room, the freedom to roam felt exhilarating. I quickly fell into a routine of walking the track each evening after work, sometimes even before dawn. The November weather was hot and delightful, and I was committed to getting fit again.

But beneath the surface of this seemingly idyllic environment lurked the dark realities of prison life. LKK had about a 90% rate of sex offenders, many of whom were some of the most heinous pedophiles in the state. I vowed to myself that I would stay out of that environment, and the best way to do that was to remain active and mobile. Working in the kitchen seven days a week and walking every night kept me from mingling with those I found repugnant.

It may sound like an overreaction, but the climate at LKK was palpable. I soon noticed groups of the worst offenders gathering, openly discussing their victims and their crimes. I was appalled and disgusted, and some of the things I heard made my skin crawl. One day, I overheard my neighbour in Lexton Cell 10, Shane, who had been banned from keeping "Best & Less" catalogues of children on his walls, discussing his sick fantasies. He used to get his "rocks off" over pictures of kids in those catalogues.

One evening, a children's show blared from the TV while I was trying to ignore the noise. I nearly vomited when I caught John and Colin sexualizing the little kids dancing in the background. "Oh, I like that one; the little one in red can be yours... I'll have the little one in yellow," John said. Rage surged within me, but I had to restrain myself. Confrontation could easily turn into a dangerous situation.

Then came the arrival of David, known as "Rosie," a notorious pedophile who had been in the media for committing horrific sexual crimes against dozens of little boys decades ago while involved in the scout movement. Soon after his arrival, I found myself working alongside him in the kitchen. Every time he opened his mouth to talk about his past, I felt my skin crawl. He was oblivious to the horror he incited; he spoke of his crimes as if he were discussing a mundane topic. "I'd do it again if I had the chance," he would casually remark, and my stomach churned at his audacity.

The other inmates in the kitchen shunned him, but I tried to remain polite, even as my insides twisted. I was aware that Rosie began to gravitate toward other pedophiles like Gavin G and Henry S, who were similarly despicable. They pounced on newcomers, especially younger ones, and the environment felt increasingly toxic.

Despite the chaos, I maintained my focus on my mission. The whispers of the Muslim brothers continued to echo in my mind. Every conversation, every interaction became a delicate balancing act as I sought to gather intel without raising suspicion. I knew I had to be strategic; these men weren't just criminals—they were potential terrorists.

Eventually, the peace I found in my routine was shattered. After working in the kitchen for over seven months, I was unexpectedly sacked. The circumstances surrounding my dismissal left a bitter taste in my mouth. I had been falsely accused of tampering with another prisoner's food, an allegation that could have serious implications for my time at LKK. The truth was simple: while assisting in the kitchen, I accidentally dropped a sausage on the floor, picked it up, dusted it off, and continued to eat it.

But Jamie, the head cook, hadn't seen anything, yet Graeme had reported me, escalating it to the higher-ups. I was called to the "Stores" office and dismissed on the spot. The feeling of injustice gnawed at me; it was a stark reminder of how fragile one's position could be in this ruthless environment.

In the weeks that followed, I felt the weight of the rumor mill churning around me. Protection prison is full of gutless, paranoid cowards who often gain satisfaction from the misery of others. One notable incident involved Craig, the biggest bloke in the jail who fancied himself the toughest. I approached him directly, confronting the whispers linking me to the situation with Simon, another inmate involved in a separate incident. I made it clear that if I continued to hear my name associated with it, I would address it.

After several weeks of investigation, I was cleared of any wrongdoing, but the ordeal left me exhausted and frustrated. I had learned another valuable lesson in the treachery that permeates prison life.

Eventually, I joined the "Bush Gang," which allowed me to engage in more meaningful work. The camaraderie among the gang members provided a sense of relief from the toxic atmosphere of the main units. We were well-received during an outing to the Avoca race track, where locals treated us with cakes and refreshments. But just as I thought I was putting the kitchen drama behind me, another issue arose.

On Monday, October 27th, during our outing, Simon returned with three cans of VB beer, a serious offense. Despite our warnings, he insisted on hiding the cans in our trailer. Later that night, as news of the beer buzzed through the jail, Simon was visibly stressed. I suggested he confess to the Senior Officer, but soon after, he was called to the Central Post and questioned about the beer found in our trailer.

Simon was transferred to Ararat the next day, and his gutless friends tried to deflect blame onto me. I was furious, and I knew I had to confront Craig about spreading my name around. The fallout from Simon's foolishness was frustrating, but I was determined to maintain my integrity amidst the chaos.

In the end, I realized that Langi Kal Kal provided both opportunities and challenges. The environment might have been more open, but the darkness of the prisoners' pasts loomed large. I had to keep my head down, gather intel on the Muslim brothers, and navigate the treacherous waters of prison life. The stakes were high, and I knew that every moment counted in my quest to ensure that the information I had reached the right people before it was too late.

Chapter 16 - Open Camp or Total Chaos?

*"In the face of uncertainty, adaptability is key." –
Unknown*

Langi Kal Kal, in theory, should have been a chance to clear my head before reintegrating back into society. An open-camp situation, as they called it, promised a semblance of freedom. However, the reality was far more sinister—a nightmare lurking behind the facade of open fields and rolling hills. I had always prided myself on maintaining a level head, but Langi presented challenges that tested my resolve like never before.

The sprawling property, with its 2,900 acres of farmland, was dotted with cows and sheep, but the real predators were the two-legged ones. Surrounded by some of the most heinous criminals—sex offenders and child molesters—the psychological toll was unbearable. While I had survived physically threatening prisons before, the daily psychological trauma of living in such a depraved environment was a different kind of torment. The 14 months I spent at LKK were some of the hardest of my life.

It might seem hard to understand, given that it was an open camp, but the presence of notorious sex offenders turned what could have been a peaceful setting into a breeding ground for fear and anxiety. I tried to keep active in both mind and body, and getting a job in the kitchen was part of my strategy. Working in the kitchen was a brilliant way to gather intel; it placed me at the center of the prison's social fabric. Everyone wanted a friend in the kitchen, and it offered me a sense of power and control amid the chaos.

At every meal, in line for the canteen, or even in the confines of my cell, I overheard conversations that made my skin crawl. Inmates reveled in recounting their sordid histories, boasting about how they groomed their five-year-old victims or fantasizing about their next targets. It was a sickening soundtrack to my daily existence.

I recall one particularly horrifying moment in my room in the Sheoak Unit. I could hear the television blaring from the lounge area, where two blokes were glued to a children's program. As the cheerful music played, Barry laughed, calling out to his companion, "Gee, I like that little one; she can be mine... which one do you want?" I felt a wave of nausea wash over me as I realized I was sharing space with men who found entertainment in the very exploitation of innocence. It was a reality that clawed at my sanity every single day.

Protection prisons, like LKK, are filled with the worst of the worst. Nearly all sex offenders, especially those who target children, are isolated from the general population for their own safety. This system, designed to protect them, inadvertently creates a haven for their twisted minds. During my time at LKK, the total muster was around 120 prisoners, with about 100 being sex offenders. As a white-collar offender, I felt like I was living in a house of horrors.

Names like John, Colin, Simon, Craig, Darren, Gavin, Shane, Ian ("Easy"), and Barry haunted my thoughts. Each of these men was a walking nightmare, carrying the burden of their heinous acts with an unsettling ease. I found myself in the kitchen one day when Rosie, a notorious pedophile, casually mentioned his past crimes while preparing food. The other inmates stared at him in disgust, but he seemed oblivious to their loathing. It was as if he reveled in the shock value, believing he was somehow showing remorse.

Working in the kitchen allowed me to position myself strategically. I would listen intently as inmates exchanged stories, often letting slip information that could be crucial. It was a double-edged sword; while I had access to valuable intel, I was also surrounded by the very individuals I loathed. The kitchen buzzed with conversations filled with bravado, tales of past exploits, and the sickening details of their crimes.

One of the most disturbing encounters I had occurred during a group meeting in the yard. Several inmates, including Gavin and Barry, were huddled together, whispering sinister plans to make a name for themselves. They were looking for new targets, new ways to assert their dominance in a place where chaos reigned. I overheard them discussing how to intimidate a newcomer—a young man who had just arrived. "We'll show him what Langi is really about," Gavin sneered, and the others laughed, their eyes glinting with malice.

I felt a chill run down my spine. The atmosphere was thick with tension, and I knew that I had to tread carefully. The last thing I wanted was to become a target for their twisted games. As I observed the group, I could feel the predator mentality grow stronger; they were circling their prey, ready to strike.

As the days turned into weeks, the environment at LKK began to wear me down. The constant undercurrent of treachery was exhausting. I had spent nearly two and a half years in prison, and the stress of my Home Detention application loomed over me like a dark cloud. Home Detention was a program for low-risk prisoners, and as a white-collar offender, I was eligible. The thought of serving the last six months of my sentence at home was a beacon of hope, but the path to that goal was fraught with uncertainty and anxiety.

Navigating the application process involved writing a detailed application and undergoing a psychological evaluation. I passed the interview in November, but the waiting game began. I had to maintain a positive mindset while staying out of the jail politics that threatened to engulf me. However, it wasn't long before the shadows of discontent crept back into my life.

Eric, an Indian bloke I had tried to befriend, was a notorious gossip. As much as I attempted to keep my distance, he was a serious pest. One day, he walked into my room, brimming with excitement about a plan to have a bloke tipped over a gambling debt. I reached my breaking point. "Eric," I snapped, "you're a scurrilous gossip who can't be trusted."

His scheme involved snitching on Dennis, known as the "TAB Manager," who took bets on everything from horse races to sports. Eric's gambling debts were piling up, and instead of confronting his issues, he wanted to drag others down with him. I warned him that his reckless behaviour could get him—or worse, me—in serious trouble.

That night, I tried to advise him to confess about the hidden beer incident from the Bush Gang. It was better to come clean than face the consequences if the officers found it themselves. But I knew the prison environment was relentless, and the fallout was inevitable.

Before long, Simon was called to the Central Post, questioned about the beer found in our trailer. The repercussions were swift; he was transferred to Ararat the next day, and his gutless friends tried to deflect the blame onto me. I was furious, knowing I had no part in his reckless actions. It was a frustrating reminder of how easily trust could be shattered in this chaotic environment.

As I navigated the treacherous waters of LKK, I was determined to maintain my integrity amidst the chaos. The prison system was a breeding ground for treachery, and I had to keep my wits about me. Each day brought new challenges, and I knew I had to adapt quickly to survive in a world filled with deceit and betrayal.

Chapter 17 - The Bombay Cabbie: Culinary Comforts in Chaos

"Food is not just fuel; it's an experience that comforts the soul." – Unknown

Having observed and listened to Eric S for nearly 12 months, I knew enough about him to understand that he would eventually turn on me, though I wasn't sure how. I kept my eyes and ears open because I knew what Eric was like—an anti-social, paranoid, gutless, psychopathic monster. He was in jail for molesting two of his stepdaughters and hailed from the Dandenong area, but I suspected he had committed similar offenses that he managed to evade. The reality of living alongside such individuals was a constant reminder of the darkness that pervaded the prison environment.

On November 20th, about a week after our argument, I returned to my room after my nightly 6 km walk, only to find a note slid under my door. The handwriting was familiar, and my heart sank as I read: "Just a friendly warning that Eric is telling people you've accessed their personal information from their phone lists. He's even told people how and where you hide the information… Watch your back with Eric because he's spreading those rumours all over the jail, including to the officers... be careful..."

While the note wasn't overtly threatening, it confirmed my suspicions about Eric's treachery. I knew the facts were incorrect; I had never done such a thing. Nevertheless, it was a heads-up about Eric's attempts to undermine me, and I had to remain vigilant.

Within hours, I discovered that Eric had gone to one of the most paranoid blokes in jail, Paul, and told him that I had personal information on him. I knew it was total nonsense, but given Paul's paranoia, I decided to confront him. On November 21st, I entered Paul's cell, reassured him that Eric's story was a lie, and that he need not worry about me. While I knew Paul would likely still believe what he wanted due to his paranoia, I wanted to address it directly.

After our conversation, I immediately notified my Case Worker and the Security Governor about the situation and Eric's little scheme. I wanted to ensure they knew the truth before anything escalated. Fortunately, they were already aware of Eric's track record as a compulsive liar, so my concerns didn't come as a surprise. They also understood my background as a model prisoner, which made the allegations against me seem out of character.

While the allegations never really gained traction, they had the potential to derail my Home Detention application, which was why I was so frustrated with Eric. Within a week of cutting him loose, he was already spinning tales about me to other prisoners, showcasing just how quickly betrayal could rear its ugly head in this environment.

As the days passed, I kept my eyes and ears open, knowing Eric wouldn't stop there. A few days later, I returned from my morning walk to find someone had thrown an entire bucket of water under my door. The rooms at LKK were carpeted, and there was about a centimeter gap under our doors—just enough for someone to tip a bucket of water through. I had left for my walk at 6:15 am, and only three blokes in our unit saw me go, with Eric being one of them. I had no doubt he was behind it.

Instead of reacting with aggression, I chose to ignore it and let it go. I made sure to tell others in the jail what he had done, knowing that would make him uncomfortable, but I never laid a hand on him. I was determined not to lower myself to his level; I needed to stay focused on my mission.

During my long walks, I had been gleaning intel from the conversations of others, staying alert to the whispers of gossip and plans that floated around me. The kitchen had become my command center, a place where I could discreetly leave information for my handlers. The toll of living in this environment was beginning to wear on me, and I felt like I was starting to crumble mentally.

The silent treatment I gave Eric was working; it was clearly bothering him. As time went on, I noticed that many inmates were turning against him, recognizing the lies he was spreading. The silent treatment was really "killing" him, and I was loving it. I simply went about my daily routine, focused on my own time, and continued my walks, leaving bits of information for my handlers whenever the opportunity arose.

Eric, in a desperate attempt to assert himself, began cooking curries in our unit. It seemed like a natural thing to do, but I knew it was his way of saying, "I'll do what I want." He knew most of the guys in our unit couldn't stand his cooking, so he started preparing curries more often and later at night. The stench of curry permeated our small unit, and he clearly didn't care how it affected anyone else.

In prison, you learn that "what goes around, comes around." While Eric was busy cooking, he had no idea that several inmates were pissing in his curry sauce and other spice jars he left in the fridge. I know it sounds disgusting, but that's what jail can be like when you upset others. I had witnessed similar antics in my time and made sure never to leave anything that could be tampered with in a communal fridge.

The irony was that Eric thought he was popular, but in reality, he was loathed by most. His cooking antics only confirmed his status as a disliked figure in the unit. The other inmates were tired of his behaviour, and the curry cooking was just the last straw. They found a twisted way to deal with him, and I couldn't help but feel a small sense of satisfaction watching his downfall.

As my handlers worked on my extraction from the system, they devised a perfect plan that wouldn't raise any suspicions. They organized a scheme for me to be considered for a program called Home Detention. It was a brilliant maneuver; someone would pose as a family member of mine, allowing me to apply to live with them under the guise of Home Detention. It was an ingenious plan, easily manipulated, and I felt a wave of relief wash over me. By now, I didn't care how they did it; I just needed out.

Finally, on December 10th, I was called to the Admin building for a video link with the Parole Board regarding my Home Detention application. A mix of nerves and anticipation coursed through me as I entered the video room. The meeting lasted about 50 minutes, covering various topics, and I felt it went reasonably well, but the anxiety weighed heavily on my mind until I finally heard the words I had been granted Home Detention.

Once I received the news, that release washed over me like a cleansing wave. I knew my time in prison was coming to an end, and while I had gathered valuable intel during my stay, the psychological toll of living in this environment had begun to chip away at my resolve. The video link took only 7-8 minutes, but it felt surreal after all the anticipation and waiting. I was finally going home.

In the next few weeks, I continued my routine, keeping to myself and avoiding unnecessary drama. The knowledge that I was leaving soon tempered my disdain for the holidays. Christmas came around, and while I hated the season, I found comfort in knowing I wouldn't be spending another one in prison.

The day itself was manageable, but I kept mostly to myself, feeling the weight of being away from family and friends. For many inmates, those in jail become their family, but I had no interest in being part of that. I believed I was doing my time, but I would never embrace the lifestyle. For those who repeatedly return to jail, I couldn't help but feel they must lack the willpower to change; it wasn't normal behaviour.

As I prepared for my transition to Home Detention, I felt a mix of gratitude and trepidation. I was ready to leave behind the chaos, the treachery, and the psychological toll that prison life had taken on me. The mission to gather intel had become a burden, and I had done enough. I was eager to embrace the freedom that awaited me outside those walls.

Chapter 18 - Release and the Post-Prison Struggle

"Freedom is not the absence of commitments, but the ability to choose." – Paulo Coelho

The day I had long awaited finally arrived, and as I navigated the last-minute paperwork and bureaucratic details at the admin office, a mix of emotions surged within me. It felt surreal. I was driven to the Trawalla Roadhouse at the front of LKK, where my handlers awaited my arrival. Seeing them in civilian clothes after so long in the dull greens of prison attire was a breath of fresh air. As we traveled down the highway, a wave of relief, excitement, and accomplishment washed over me—I had survived jail, and I was glad to put that chapter behind me. I knew I would never return.

For anyone curious about what it's like to get out, I can honestly say that not once did I think about the jail or any of the inmates I had encountered. The idea of missing "friends" from inside is ludicrous; those people were merely acquaintances who played a role in my life during a difficult time. It was work; it was my duty.

However, the impact of incarceration lingered like a heavy fog. While leaving prison and surviving my undercover assignment was a significant achievement, I had to focus on readjusting to normal life. The transition wouldn't be easy; I needed to desensitize myself to everyday experiences and relationships. Stepping back into a world that felt foreign after years of confinement weighed heavily on me, and the psychological trauma of prison life clung to my psyche.

In the weeks following my release, I was thrust into a whirlwind of debriefing meetings with my handlers. I had to relive, memorize, and explain all the intel I had gathered over the two years during my mission—an exhausting process that required me to recount harrowing details about the Muslim brothers and the terrorist cells. Additionally, I had to provide information about Anthony D's murder and the atrocious killing of Angelique D. Each session felt like I was peeling back layers of my own trauma, exposing raw wounds that had barely begun to heal.

The intensity of these meetings was crushing. I had had enough; I was exhausted from the stress of it all. The final release and getting out should have felt like a victory, but instead, it was a reminder of the nightmare that had unfolded over what was supposed to be a 12-month mission but had stretched into more than double that. Each recollection felt like a weight pressing down on my chest, making it difficult to breathe.

This entire experience had changed me forever. The treachery I had witnessed among inmates eroded my trust in people. I had seen how quickly alliances could shift, how easily betrayal could rear its ugly head. The psychological toll of living amongst individuals capable of such heinous acts left scars that would take time to fade. I grappled with the fear of death that had shadowed me during my time undercover, an ever-present reminder of the dangers that lurked in the criminal world.

I knew it was my obligation and duty to provide this information, yet as I sat in those meetings, I often felt like I was breaking down psychologically and emotionally. The pressure to recall every detail, to ensure nothing was overlooked, was immense. The memories of the chaos I had witnessed in prison, the vile conversations I had overheard, haunted me.

Personal safety was now a concern, too. The fear of retribution from those I had encountered in the criminal world loomed over me like a dark cloud. I had to remain vigilant while re-establishing my place in society. The skills I had honed in prison—keeping my guard up and staying aware—were now crucial in navigating this new phase of my life.

During my long walks in the weeks leading up to my release, I had used the opportunity to glean intelligence from others while discreetly leaving bits of information for my handlers. Those walks served a dual purpose: they allowed me to engage with others while collecting and sending vital intel about ongoing threats related to my undercover work. Now, however, it felt like a distant memory, overshadowed by the pressure of my current reality.

As I settled back into daily life, I focused on reconnecting with my family and friends, but I was acutely aware of the trauma I had experienced and the adjustments I needed to make. Simple interactions became daunting. I had to relearn how to engage in normal conversations, navigate social situations, and rebuild relationships that had been strained or altered during my time away.

Moments of discomfort were frequent. Loud noises or sudden movements could trigger anxiety, and I often felt the need to assess my surroundings—a habit formed during my time in confinement. I was conscious of my heightened alertness and the need to recalibrate my responses to a world that felt both familiar and alien.

My handlers assured me that they were working on my extraction from the system, and their support was invaluable. But the pressure to ensure that justice was served weighed heavily on me. I knew that the information I had gathered could be pivotal in prosecuting others who posed a threat. The knowledge that I still had a role to play in the fight against these dangers kept me focused, even as the stress threatened to overwhelm me.

As I navigated this new phase, I reminded myself that I had the tools to succeed. I was determined to reclaim my life while continuing to honor my commitment to my undercover work. Each day brought its challenges, but I faced them with the understanding that the road ahead would require resilience, patience, and a willingness to confront my fears.

The challenge of reintegration was daunting, but I was committed to overcoming it. I knew that the skills I had developed in prison—resilience, determination, and the ability to adapt—would serve me well as I embarked on this new chapter in my life. The experience had scarred me, but it had also forged a stronger, more resolute version of myself. I was ready to transition into the world outside, to face the challenges of normal life, and to ensure that I remained a part of the fight against the very threats I had encountered during my time undercover.

Chapter 19 - Turning Trials into Triumphs

"The greatest glory in living lies, not in never falling, but in rising every time we fall." – Nelson Mandela

I've been asked many questions about my time in jail and whether it has had any effect on me. While I managed to survive the experience, I am certainly not the same person I was when I entered the system. In many ways, I believe I'm a better person for it, but the lessons I learned were hard-fought. Nothing could have prepared me for the harsh realities I faced during my time behind bars.

Jail is a soul-destroying place, filled with heartache and despair. Despite the challenges, I'm proud of my ability to navigate that environment while maintaining my composure and focus on my goals. There were incredibly low periods, and I certainly experienced moments of depression, but I was determined to stay positive in mind and body, even when the weight of my mission felt overwhelming.

My time in jail was filled with trauma, witnessing violence and the darker sides of humanity that left lasting marks on my psyche. Through it all, I held onto my purpose: to gather crucial intelligence on the Muslim brothers and other potential threats to the community. The knowledge that my efforts could lead to justice for victims and their families fueled my resolve. Seeing Anthony D receive an 18-year sentence for murder brought me a sense of satisfaction, knowing that I played a part in ensuring justice for that young woman's family.

Yet, the profound impact of this experience weighed heavily on me as I transitioned back into normal life. The trauma lingered, and adjusting to everyday life was a challenge. I had to relearn how to navigate relationships, desensitizing myself to normal social interactions that felt overwhelming after my time inside.

Returning to the outside world meant facing the reality of my experiences while attempting to reintegrate into society. I needed to readjust to the simple things—conversations, social cues, and daily routines—while managing the stress that came with it. I was a clean-skin, unaccustomed to the challenges of reestablishing myself after such an intense period away.

Throughout my time in jail, I had learned to be observant and strategic, skills that would serve me well as I continued my undercover role. The next phases of my mission would require careful planning and execution. My personal safety was a primary concern; I had to remain vigilant about potential threats from individuals I had encountered during my time undercover.

But the secrecy of my mission loomed large, adding another layer of complexity to my reintegration. I longed to share my story, to vent my struggles and seek comfort from friends or family. Yet, the weight of confidentiality pressed down on me. I knew that sharing even the smallest detail could endanger not only my life but the lives of my loved ones. The thought of retribution from those I had investigated haunted me, and the knowledge of forthcoming court cases and potential serious convictions kept me silent. It was a heavy burden, one that gnawed at my insides.

The addition of this secrecy played on my mind, amplifying my stress levels. I wanted to celebrate my success in a way—after all, I had done what I was trained to do, succeeded, and lived to tell the tale. But the victory felt hollow when I could not share it with anyone. The isolation of my experience deepened, and I felt trapped in a silence that was both protective and suffocating.

As I navigated the complexities of readjusting to life outside, I recognized the importance of seeking support. I began talking to counselors to help process the trauma and re-establish my mental well-being. I was committed to not letting my experiences define me or hold me back from achieving my goals.

I faced challenges in finding a routine that felt normal while still dealing with the aftereffects of prison life. The stress and anxiety I carried were constant reminders of my time inside, but I was resolute in my determination to reclaim my life. I focused on building relationships with family and friends, knowing that their support would be crucial in my journey.

The process of reintegration was not something I could rush; it would take time and patience. I was grateful for the opportunity to continue my work while taking steps to rebuild my life. I wanted to ensure that my efforts in gathering intelligence would lead to meaningful change and justice for those affected by crime.

Ultimately, I knew that the experiences I had endured would shape me, but they would not define my future. I was determined to move forward, using my past as a foundation for a more purposeful life, committed to making a positive impact in the world around me. The journey ahead would be fraught with challenges, but I was ready to face them head-on, carrying with me the lessons learned in the darkest of places.

Chapter 20 - Lessons from Loss: Embracing the Journey

"Sometimes, the hardest lessons to learn are the ones that teach us the most." – Unknown

I've been asked many questions about my time in jail and whether it has had any effect on me. While I managed to survive the experience, I am certainly not the same person I was when I entered the system. In many ways, I believe I've become a better person, but the cost of that transformation has been steep. Some of life's lessons are hard-learned, and nothing could have prepared me for the harsh realities I faced during my time there.

Jail is a soul-destroying place, filled with heartache and despair. Yet, amid the chaos, I take pride in my resilience and my ability to navigate that environment while staying focused on my goals. Throughout my time, I was driven by a singular purpose—to gather crucial intelligence on the Muslim brothers and other potential threats to our community. Knowing that my efforts contributed to the safety of others and played a part in ensuring justice for victims and their families provided a sense of satisfaction that helped sustain me through the darkest moments.

One of the hardest challenges I faced while in jail was maintaining a positive mindset. I've always been an optimistic person, and I tried to hold onto that light even during my lowest points. With dreams comes hope, and I firmly believe that having hope is essential for achieving one's goals. I understood that the time spent in jail could not define me; instead, I would use my experiences to build a new future.

However, as I transitioned back into normal life, I found myself grappling with the weight of my experiences. The impact of that time in prison lingered like a shadow, and I had to confront the emotional scars that accompanied it. Adjusting to the everyday world felt overwhelming at times, especially while managing the stress and trauma that I carried within me. I was acutely aware that re-establishing normal relationships and routines would require time, patience, and immense effort.

In my journey of reintegration, I focused on rebuilding connections with family and friends. Their support was a lifeline, essential as I navigated this new phase of life. Yet, I felt a deep-seated struggle within me—the secrecy surrounding my mission weighed heavily on my heart. The knowledge that I could not share my story or vent my feelings to those I cared about added to the burden. It was excruciating to remain silent about my experiences, knowing that lives could be at risk, especially mine and my family's. I wanted to celebrate my success in a way; I had done what I was trained to do, succeeded, and lived to tell the tale. But the silence was suffocating, preventing me from finding solace in the camaraderie of those around me.

I also understood that the skills I had developed in prison—resilience, determination, and strategic thinking—would serve me well as I continued my mission to gather intelligence and ensure that those who posed a danger were held accountable. The challenges of re-entering normal life were daunting, but I remained committed to my purpose. I was determined to ensure that my efforts in gathering intelligence would lead to meaningful change and justice for those impacted by crime.

Processing the trauma of my experiences became a priority. I began to seek support from counselors, recognizing that it was essential for my mental well-being. This journey of healing was both necessary and difficult; I was adjusting to a world that felt both familiar and foreign. I wanted to ensure that the scars of my experiences did not dictate my future or define who I was.

Throughout this process, gratitude emerged as a powerful force within me. I felt thankful for the opportunity to contribute to my community, to do my part in the fight against crime. My conscience was clear, knowing that I had acted for the greater good. While the memories of my time in jail would always linger, I was determined to use them as a foundation for a more purposeful life.

As I moved forward, I understood that the path to reintegration would not be without its difficulties. The emotional toll of secrecy and the weight of unshared stories would continue to challenge me. However, I was equipped with the knowledge and support necessary to navigate this new reality. I remained focused on my goals, determined to contribute positively to society and ensure that justice was served for those affected by crime.

In the end, I knew that while I had endured a challenging experience, it had also given me a profound sense of purpose. I was committed to making a difference, and I believed that my journey could inspire others who faced similar challenges. I was ready to embrace this new chapter in my life, determined to leave the past behind while forging a brighter future for myself and my community.

Chapter 21 - Footprints of Failure and Success

"Success is not the absence of failure; it's the persistence through failure." – *Aisha Tyler*

Throughout my journey, I've often reflected on the profound impact of my experiences. My time in jail, though challenging, has undeniably shaped me and propelled me toward success in my undercover operation. The intelligence I gathered during my mission played a crucial role in preventing severe terrorist offenses in Melbourne and other parts of Australia. This accomplishment fills me with immense pride, knowing that I contributed to the safety of my community and upheld my duty to protect those around me.

The satisfaction of being able to honor my family and my father while serving my country is a feeling I cherish deeply. I recognize that my efforts, though small in the grand scheme, were part of a larger mission orchestrated by the Federal and State Intelligence Services. It was a privilege to have had the opportunity to serve in this capacity, and I approach my work with gratitude for the chance to make a difference.

While I faced significant challenges during my time in jail, I am determined to focus on the positives and the invaluable lessons learned. I understand that the psychological effects of my experiences can linger, but I am committed to confronting these challenges head-on. The trauma I endured and the experiences of prison life have changed me, but they will not define my future.

As I reintegrate into normal life, I acknowledge that some relationships have shifted or even been lost. Many people assumed the worst during my absence, and though I was fulfilling a critical role as an undercover operative, they could not see the full picture. It's disheartening to know that only a small number of individuals understood my purpose while many chose to walk away. However, I have no regrets; the mission had to be completed, and I am proud to have played my part in it.

Resilience in the face of adversity has become a cornerstone of my character. As I navigate this new chapter, I remind myself of Winston Churchill's words: "Success is not final, failure is not fatal: It is the courage to continue that counts." Each setback has become an opportunity for growth, and I am determined to seize every chance to build my future.

In rebuilding my life, I'm also focused on creating a positive legacy for my children and grandchildren. Life is worth living, and I want to leave behind a good footprint. I understand that challenges lie ahead, but I am committed to facing them with the strength and resilience I have developed through my experiences.

My journey has taught me that the path to success is often paved with trials. It is those trials that shape our character and prepare us for greater challenges. I believe that every experience, no matter how difficult, can be transformed into a stepping stone toward a brighter future. I am grateful for the lessons learned and the strength gained during my time undercover and in prison.

As I move forward, I will continue to honor my commitment to community safety. The challenges I faced have only strengthened my resolve to contribute positively to society. I am proud of what I have accomplished and remain focused on a future filled with purpose and meaning. I refuse to let the shadows of my past dictate my future; instead, I will use them as fuel to propel myself forward.

In conclusion, I choose to view my experiences as a testament to resilience and determination. I am ready to embrace the opportunities ahead, armed with the knowledge that success is not just about the destination but also about the journey itself. Life is a continuous process of growth, and I am committed to making the most of every moment, using my past as a foundation to forge a brighter future for myself and those I love.

Chapter 22 - Resilience in the Face of Adversity

Every day you spend is one day you can never get back! Time is precious, and it's essential to make the most of every moment.

Reflecting on my journey, I recognize the importance of using my experiences to build a solid foundation for future success. Life presents us all with challenges, but it's how we respond to these challenges that truly defines our path forward. I believe that every hurdle is not just an obstacle but an opportunity for growth—a chance to learn and a test of our determination to succeed.

Success is often born out of resilience and the ability to rise after setbacks. I've learned that life is about taking proactive steps toward our goals, no matter how daunting they may seem. Each day offers us 86,400 seconds, and it's crucial to use that time wisely. I understand now that preparation is key in navigating the unpredictable changes life throws at us.

One of the most significant lessons I've taken from my experiences is the immense value of surrounding myself with positive influences. The environment we cultivate plays a vital role in shaping our success and overall well-being. By connecting with good people and mentors who inspire and motivate me, I can create opportunities for growth and achievement that might otherwise remain out of reach.

Mentorship is a powerful tool for personal and professional development, as well as for healing. A mentor provides guidance, shares wisdom, and encourages us to reach our full potential. I firmly believe in the importance of selecting mentors who embody the values and success I aspire to achieve. Their insights can illuminate the path ahead, helping me navigate challenges while remaining true to my principles and purpose.

As I look toward the future, I am filled with optimism. I recognize that while the road ahead may present obstacles, I am equipped to face them. The journey I've undertaken has instilled in me a renewed sense of purpose and clarity. I am committed to making the most of the opportunities that come my way, and I intend to contribute positively to my community, ensuring that my efforts leave a lasting impact.

While relationships may have shifted during my time away, I am grateful for the bonds that have strengthened through adversity. The true measure of friendship reveals itself in difficult times, and I am fortunate to have a small circle of supporters who believe in me. Together, we create a network of encouragement that fosters growth and success, lifting each other up as we navigate our individual paths.

I understand that life is a continuous journey of learning and evolution. Each experience, whether positive or challenging, contributes to the person I am becoming. I strive to make choices that align with my values and aspirations, ensuring that my actions reflect the legacy I wish to leave for my children and grandchildren.

As I embark on this new chapter, I am reminded of the words of Ralph Waldo Emerson: "Our greatest glory is not in never failing, but in rising up every time we fail." This sentiment encapsulates my approach to life. It's not about avoiding challenges; it's about how we respond to them and the strength we derive from resilience.

With gratitude for the opportunities I have been given and the lessons I've learned, I look forward to building a future filled with purpose and promise. I am determined to make a positive impact, honour my family, and uphold the values that have shaped me into the person I am today.

In conclusion, while I acknowledge the challenges that lie ahead, I am confident in my ability to navigate them. I will embrace each day with hope and determination, knowing that every moment is a chance to create a brighter future.

Life is indeed worth living, and I am wholeheartedly committed to making the most of it.

Chapter 23 - If It Is To Be, It's Up To Me: Taking Charge

"You are the master of your destiny. You can influence, direct, and control your own environment." – Napoleon Hill

Every day is a new opportunity, a chance to make meaningful choices and create a positive impact. I've come to understand that time is invaluable; it's something we can never reclaim. What we do with that time defines our journey and shapes our future. It's a reminder that our lives are a series of moments, and how we choose to fill those moments can determine the legacy we leave behind.

As I reflect on my experiences, I recognize the profound impact of my undercover operation. The intelligence I gathered not only contributed to preventing serious threats in Melbourne and across Australia, but it also ensured that justice was served for those who needed it most. Knowing that I played a part in keeping my community safe fills me with immense pride and satisfaction. It reinforces my belief that every effort counts, and that positive actions can lead to significant change. As Gandhi once said, "Be the change that you wish to see in the world."

I am deeply grateful for the opportunity to honor my family through my work. Their unwavering support has been instrumental in my journey, and I am committed to making a lasting, positive difference in their lives and in the lives of others. The challenges I faced were not in vain; they paved the way for growth, resilience, and a deeper understanding of my purpose.

Success is rarely a straight path; it often requires hard work, perseverance, and the willingness to face obstacles head-on. I wholeheartedly believe that every setback is an opportunity for growth. Each challenge I encountered has taught me valuable lessons that I carry forward. As I move ahead, my focus will be on the strengths gained from my experiences, shaping a future that reflects my values and aspirations.

Surrounding myself with positive influences is essential to my ongoing success. I understand the importance of having mentors and role models who inspire and challenge me to reach my full potential. Their guidance is invaluable as I navigate future endeavours and strive to make a positive impact in my community. As the saying goes, "If you want to go fast, go alone. If you want to go far, go together."

Reflecting on the past, I acknowledge the challenges I faced, including individuals like Anthony D, who ultimately faced the consequences of their actions. The truth has a way of surfacing, and the system works to ensure that justice prevails. I find solace in knowing that my contributions have played a role in holding those who threaten our safety accountable. The journey may have been difficult, but it was necessary, and it has shaped me into who I am today.

As I step into this new chapter, I am filled with hope and determination. I am excited about the opportunities that lie ahead and the chance to create a meaningful legacy for my family. The values instilled in me by my parents guide my actions and decisions. Their courage and resilience serve as a constant reminder of what it means to honor family and community. I am inspired by their strength and motivated to carry their legacy forward.

I believe that together, we can foster an environment of positivity and support. Life is not about perfection; it's about progress and the willingness to learn from our experiences. I am committed to embracing the journey, celebrating successes, and learning from challenges. Each step I take is a testament to the resilience I have developed, and I am eager to share that strength with others.

In closing, I want to emphasize that each of us has the power to make a difference, no matter how small. The light we bring into the world can illuminate even the darkest corners. As I continue on my path, I am dedicated to creating a brighter future, not just for myself, but for my children and grandchildren. It's time to embrace the possibilities ahead and to live with purpose and passion.

As I move forward, I carry with me the lessons of the past, the strength of my family, and the unwavering belief that together, we can create a better tomorrow. My journey has taught me that while the road may be long and fraught with challenges, it is also filled with opportunities for growth, healing, and transformation. With determination in my heart and hope in my soul, I am ready to take charge of my future and make a meaningful impact on the world around me.

Final Statement

As I conclude this journey, I wish to reflect on the profound experiences I encountered during my time as an undercover operative. My mission was not just a personal endeavour; it was a commitment to doing the right thing for my country, my community, and, most importantly, to honor my family, particularly my father. The risks I faced were tremendous, and the situations I encountered were fraught with danger and life-threatening challenges.

The courage exhibited by my wife and son throughout this ordeal was nothing short of extraordinary. They supported me, fully aware of the peril I was undertaking, with only a handful of trusted individuals privy to my true mission. This discretion was crucial; any further disclosure could have jeopardized not only my safety but the integrity of the operation itself. Their unwavering faith in me and our shared commitment to the greater good kept me grounded during the most trying times.

The stakes were high as I navigated a world filled with deceit, treachery, and violence. Throughout this mission, I was able to thwart multiple potential terrorist attacks that could have targeted our community and country. The success of this operation is a testament to the dedication and bravery of those involved, including the intelligence and legal communities, my handlers, and the few family members who stood by me without question. Their unwavering support in the face of severe stress was invaluable, and I am deeply grateful for their understanding of the importance of the work I was doing.

This experience has profoundly changed me as a person. Surviving in jail under such horrendous conditions exposed me to sights and sounds that haunt me—things I cannot unsee or discuss. The impact of this journey extends far beyond the pages of this book, which reflects only a tiny fraction of what I experienced and the individuals I came into contact with. I am acutely aware that detailing more names and activities could endanger others involved in this complex web of operations.

I hope this book offers insights into life behind bars: the treachery, the lies, and the deceit; the appalling living conditions; and the constant tension that defines prison life. My goal was to demystify some of the myths surrounding the prison system and provide an authentic portrayal of the environment I endured. It is my hope that readers can cultivate a greater understanding of the complexities of human behaviour and the circumstances that often lead people down dark paths.

As I look to the future, I carry with me a renewed sense of purpose and a commitment to contribute positively to society. I am grateful for the opportunity to have played a role in a mission that, while dangerous, was essential for the safety of others. The lessons learned from this experience will remain with me, guiding my path forward. I am more aware than ever of the importance of kindness, compassion, and understanding in our interactions with one another. Life is too short to hold onto judgments; we must strive to uplift each other, recognizing that everyone has their own battles to fight.

In closing, I extend my heartfelt gratitude to everyone who supported me along this arduous journey. Thank you to the intelligence community, the legal professionals, my handlers, and, most importantly, my family and friends. Your belief in the importance of this mission and your strength during this time made all the difference. Together, we have contributed to a safer future, and for that, I am eternally grateful.

As we move forward together, let us cultivate an atmosphere of support and understanding, extending kindness to those around us. It is through our collective efforts that we can create a brighter, safer world for generations to come.

Author's Note on Naming Individuals

In this book, I have made the deliberate choice to reveal the real names of a select few individuals referenced throughout my book. However, I must emphasize that I have intentionally withheld the names of key figures—particularly the serious Muslim brothers and suspected terrorists—whose identities remain shrouded in secrecy. This decision is not made lightly; it is a matter of national security.

To disclose the full names of these dangerous individuals could jeopardize ongoing investigations and compromise future court proceedings. The ramifications of such exposure extend far beyond personal safety, threatening the very fabric of our national security and the lives of countless innocent people. The stakes are high, and I cannot allow the pursuit of a sensational narrative to overshadow the imperative of safeguarding lives.

Moreover, I am acutely aware of the need to protect the identities and security of my family, my handlers, and others involved in this intricate web of operations. The most perilous individuals remain nameless to prevent drawing any further attention to them or to those connected with me. In addition, I have taken the precaution of altering the names of my family members, not out of desire for anonymity, but out of necessity for their protection.

I implore you, the reader, to understand and respect these critical considerations as you engage with this narrative. The shadows of my experiences are not merely stories; they are reminders of the very real dangers that lurk in the world. Your comprehension of the gravity of these omissions is greatly appreciated as we navigate this complex and often treacherous landscape together.

Names (in no particular order)

Abdul NB	Abdul NB
Lorenzo F	Lorenzo Favata
Adam	Ahmed Ibrahim
Alex L	Alex Lazarides
David M	David Mummery
Anthony D	Anthony Dutton
Meeso	David Meeson
Roz S	Roz Smith (MRC Governor)
Dave F	Dave Foster (SMU)
Tom C	Tom Cat (Ararat)

Frank B	Frank Bort (Ararat)
Rodney P	Rodney Petersen (Ararat)
James H	James Harrison (Ararat)
Mark AJ	Mark Anthony Jewell
Kasey K	Kasey Kowski
Peter R	Peter Reid
Craig D	Craig Delgado
Simon S Rapist)	Simon Smith (Melton Granny
Eric S	Eric Roland Smith (LKK)
Graham K	Graham Kelly (LKK)
Barry G	Barry Garret (LKK)
Paul C	Paul Caine (LKK)
Jamie M	Jamie Myers (LKK)
Ian C	Ian Collie (LKK)
John Mc	John McFee (LKK)
Colin R	Colin Ryrie (LKK)

Poems from My Journey

In this section, I have included a selection of poems that I wrote during my time inside. These poems serve as a profound reflection of my state of mind and psyche at various moments throughout this incredible journey. They offer readers another valuable insight into my experiences, emotions, and the challenges I faced as I navigated the complexities of my undercover mission.

I want to clarify that I have deliberately changed the names of individuals mentioned in these poems, particularly when referencing my family or loved ones. This decision was made with their safety and privacy in mind, as it is essential to protect their identities for obvious reasons. All references to my love, my wife, and my son are presented without their real names to ensure their continued safety and security.

I invite you to engage with these poems, which encapsulate the depth of my experiences and emotions during this extraordinary chapter of my life

The Nights Are So Lonely

My mind is screaming, my head feels about to explode,
Another nightmare haunts me it's the end of the road.
Each dream is the same; I always die,
I wake in a cold sweat, tears in my eye.
But reality hits—I'm not at home,
Lying in my jail bed, so utterly alone.
No one to comfort me, no girl to hug,
I pull the blanket tight, trying to feel snug.
I'm frightened I'm scared, unsure what to do,
Wishing I were at home, lying next to you.
Instead, I'm here, staring at the ceiling,
Wondering what it is I'm meant to be feeling.
It's pitch black in here, silent as a grave,
I long for your presence, your warmth I crave.
The clock's out of sight; I don't know the time,
In the dead of night, I'm lost in the rhyme.
It's times like these that make you feel frail,
No matter how tough, you're alone in jail.
You're not meant to cry; you're told to be strong,
But lying here in darkness just feels so wrong.
As I lay in the stillness, nothing in sight,

I strive to hold on, to make it through the night.

My mind races on, I seek thoughts that uplift,

I remember the good times, the moments that gift.

I think of my son, those days by the stream,

But my heart aches for you; you're part of my dream.

You're not just my lover; you're my guiding light,

In the midst of this darkness, you make everything right.

So I close my eyes, let sleep take its hold,

With visions of you, my heart turns to gold.

Your love fills the void, a comforting thought,

If you could see me now, you'd know what I've sought.

I drift off once more as the night starts to pass,

Though this won't be the last,

I'll find strength at last.

22 Hour Lockdown

It's 2:30 am, and I'm wide awake,
Wondering just how much more I can take.
A quick glance around, reality sets in,
For a moment, I forgot the slot I'm in.
The cell is dark, cold, and confined,
Loneliness and isolation weigh on my mind.
To cope, I dream of places I'd rather be,
But most of all, I wish my girl was here with me.
It hasn't been easy; it's been a tough year,
There have been moments filled with many tears.
I know it's hard; it's not meant to be fun.
Yet I find hope knowing this is just a stage I've begun.
I dream of the day when I'll settle down,
Once more with my wife, wearing love's crown.
I focus on the good things that bring me cheer,
And I spend my time writing letters, holding her near.
She's gorgeous and funny, a true delight,
I wish I could share more of her light.
With a great sense of humour, she brightens my day,
If you saw her, you'd surely say, "What a ray!"
As you can see, I'm missing my girl,

Just thinking of her sends my mind in a whirl.
When I'm with her, I feel an immense pride,
At times, I wish I could yell her name far and wide.
But for now, I'm here, all alone in this place,
In a few hours, morning will bring a new face.
Soon there'll be a knock; it's breakfast, I know,
Three pieces of cold toast—oh, what a show!
At 8 AM, I'll be allowed out for a walk,
With two others, we'll share a brief talk.
A chat with the blokes, a phone call to make,
We're caged like chickens, but we'll do what it takes.
The two hours pass, and our time is up,
Back to lockdown, no more coffee cup.
Two hours a day, that's all I can claim,
Then it's back to my cell, locked in the game.
There's little to do, maybe a letter to write,
I gaze out my window, searching for light.
Surrounded by concrete and razor wire near,
I sit and wonder what's out there, unclear.
I miss the simple things; it's hard to explain,
The shower, my own pillow, the comforts I gain.
A splash of aftershave to feel like me,
But in this place, it's an impossible plea.

Meals come and go through the slot in the door,
What they serve isn't much, it's hard to ignore.
The staff keep it moving, they're just doing their job,
There's Stewie, Mr. Lee, and a guy named Rob.
But I won't feel sorry; I own where I stand,
I don't need tears from others, I'll take my own hand.
I must stay positive, look ahead with hope,
Until the day I walk out and back to my home.
Each day I'm in here brings me closer to free,
To see my friends and the world waiting for me.
But what I truly yearn for is my girl's soft embrace,
To see her, to kiss her, to feel her grace.
As I ponder the boredom that fills up my day,
There are just a few more things I want to say.
My girl is my everything; she is my life!

Doing Time

Sitting all alone in here,
Out my cell window, I peer.
Concrete walls surround me it's a heavy weight,
Wondering how much longer I can wait.
I'm in jail, and it's not meant to be fun,
But sometimes I ponder what I've done.
Though the days are long, I know I must be tough,
Crying won't help; it's no use to bluff.
I'm on my own, just another face,
A reminder now of my past embrace.
Musters to endure and boring clothes to wear,
Occasionally, they let me cut my hair.
The system's slow, nothing happens fast,
I can wait for weeks; it feels like a cast.
A visit from friends is a true blessing,
But just one hour leaves me second-guessing.
While drugs are an issue, I stand my ground,
At least here, no pressure can be found.
I've learned to watch the words that I say,
For the wrong move could lead my life astray.
The hardest part is that some call this home,

With friends around, they're never alone.
It's hard for me; I'm not used to this strife,
I grew up in a family filled with love and life.
So here I am, facing this jail,
Determined to stay positive and prevail.
I write to my friends, sending letters with care,
A few words to let them know I'm still here.
There's my mum, my sister, and special friends,
Their voices lift me; their love never ends.
They cheer me on, keeping me sane,
Their unwavering support eases the pain.
What sets me apart is the love that I find,
The people who care, always so kind.
It's a reality check, through the loneliness I tread,
But their love fuels my spirit, keeping me fed.
I cherish the simple things I once took for granted,
The lessons instilled by my parents, so planted.
Love, respect, kindness, freedom—values we know,
These seeds of wisdom are what help me grow.
As I ponder my journey for yet another day,
There are just a few things I want to convey.
It's the love and support of my family and friends,
That keeps my spirit alive, and my hope never ends.

Until Forever

I've never known a love like yours,
Nor dreamed it could be true,
But every time I kiss your lips,
I feel the magic of love anew.
With hair like silk and lips so tender,
Each moment with you makes my heart surrender.
I couldn't live, I couldn't breathe,
Without you by my side,
Never will I let you go,
My love will never hide.
In my heart, you'll always dwell,
From now until forever,
No matter what, no matter where,
Together we'll weather.
I love you deeply, endlessly,
In every breath I take,
With you, my love, I've found my home,
A bond that will never break.

Another Day in Paradise

It's nearly 8 o'clock; it's lockdown time,

So I'll write a poem and make it rhyme.

Not much to do, maybe a book to read,

Or have a snack, though it's one I don't need.

It's another night in jail, and it's not much fun,

But I'm serving my time for the choices I've done.

No point in looking back; it's a waste of breath,

I've got to accept it, learn from this test.

I have a little while to reflect and grow,

Hoping when I'm done, I'll regain some respect, you know.

In the meantime, I've got another night to get through,

And I'll spend much of it thinking of you.

You're on my mind; you're always there,

I know you love me, and you truly care.

I'm not seeking excuses or asking for pity,

It's my fault I'm here; I was truly silly.

So here I am, I'll pick up a book,

There might be something on the TV—let's take a look.

I could chat with my cellmate or write a letter or two,

But I'd rather be lost in thoughts of you.

Sometimes it's hard; there are three of us here,

Needing some space, wishing to shed a tear.
But crims are meant to be tough; we're not meant to cry,
It's just the way it is; I don't question why.
No use feeling sorry for myself, as I said,
I may as well settle down and rest my head.
Morning will come; it's a new day ahead,
A few blokes are getting out—lucky are they, instead.
For me, it's just another day in this place,
Hoping for letters from friends, a warm embrace.
That's always a highlight, one of the few,
A way to stay connected, to keep up with the news.
But other than that, there's not much to see,
So I'll spend tomorrow, thinking of thee.
You're what get's me through each long day,
You're my only one; that's what I want to say.
It's time to close my eyes and dream of just you,
Imagining a future that's bright and true.

Another Day In Jail

Another day in jail, where fun's hard to find,
Sometimes the weight on my shoulders feels heavy and blind.
There are programs to join, things to pursue,
But nothing compares to my longing for you.
You're cute, witty, and ever so kind,
The girl that any man would be lucky to find.
When I get my chance, I'll be knocking at your door,
But for now, I'm inside, longing for more.
Every day that I think of you brings a smile,
Though I'm still in here for a little while.
There are moments when life feels completely lost,
But I'd give anything just to be with you at any cost.
You're my girl, my soul-mate; I'll do all I can,
I hope you feel the same, understand my plan.
I know there have been tears along this way,
But when I get out, it'll be a brighter day.
I'll work hard to get back on my feet,
Even if it means I have to break a sweat to compete.
I know it's worth it to have you back near,
I promise you'll see, I'll conquer my fear.
For now, I have another day to get through,

And I'll spend most of it thinking of you.
The good times we've shared and those yet to come,
These thoughts fill my heart, make my spirit hum.
As I said before, I've stumbled and strayed,
But dreaming of you keeps my hope unafraid.
I better stop now and finish my chores,
I hope you're reading this; I'm not being a bore.
The last thing I want to say before this I send,
Is that you're my partner, my love, my best friend.

Away From My Love

I'm away from my love; I feel lost and helpless,
Shattered and depressed, in a state that's so restless.
Sitting by myself, feeling all alone,
Like a dog without its cherished bone.
My love, she's wonderful; she is my life,
Without her beside me, I'm engulfed in strife.
I can't explain the emptiness I bear,
Not having her with me feels profoundly unfair.
Why does my heart ache, feeling pierced through?
Why are my eyes brimming with tears, so true?
Why does my head pound, feeling like it will burst?
Is it because I'm away from my love, who always comes first?
It's clear now; the penny has finally dropped,
There's only one way to make this heartache stop.
I need to find my girl, my only true love,
Lindy, my partner, my angel from above.

Jail Is Not Fun

Yes, the rules and regulations are scattered all around,
Though we have some space, it's a heavy ground.
Jail is tough; it's not meant to be fun,
In some areas, the officers carry guns.
All day long, you watch every word you say,
One wrong slip, and you could pay the price today.
There's plenty of nonsense, many stories unfold,
Some guys act tough, but they're really just bold.
One thing I've learned in this short span of time,
The best course of action is to avoid a whine.
Jail is hard; doing your time can be lonely,
Especially when you're away from your family.
In my case, I have a beautiful wife at home,
Sitting here thinking of her, I often feel alone.
It's painful for me; she's the love of my life,
Lindy, that's my gorgeous wife.
She's my best friend, the one who makes me proud,
I wish I could tell everyone, scream it out loud.
She's my wife and my lover; she means everything to me,
Her beautiful lips, her cute smile—oh, how they shine so free.
For now, I'll keep dreaming and serving my time,

Eventually, I'll reach the top of the mountain I climb.
But no matter how many peaks I conquer and run,
The battle isn't won until I'm home with my wife and son.

Attachments and Sketches

In this section, I have included a series of attachments and sketches that provide additional context to my undercover mission. These documents offer a glimpse into various aspects of prison life, detailing everything from eating arrangements and sleeping conditions to working life within the system. You will find canteen shopping lists, notes I took while gathering intelligence on Anthony Dutton and his murder, sketches of actual prison cells from various facilities, and even a song I wrote during my time there.

While some of this material may not resonate with every reader, I hope it serves as an insightful glimpse into my journey. These attachments reflect my state of mind, my relentless effort to maintain my sanity, and my commitment to keeping my mind sharp and active amidst the stress, anxiety, and pressures of fulfilling my mission. They illustrate my immersion in the culture and community of the prison system, showcasing the unique experiences and challenges I faced along the way.

I invite you to explore these insights and discover another layer of my story, one that complements the narrative shared throughout the book.

Sketch of Melbourne Remand Centre

This was me taking a look at the Melbourne Remand Centre (MRC) which was in Truganina. Once people leave the Melbourne Assessment Prison in Spencer St, they get taken to the MRC. It is an absolute pressure cooker because it is full of tension and heat because most crims have just been arrested and are often awaiting their fate in court and naturally it is a challenge to survive. Every day, there were fights and stabbings and retribution handed out. It was tense to say the least.

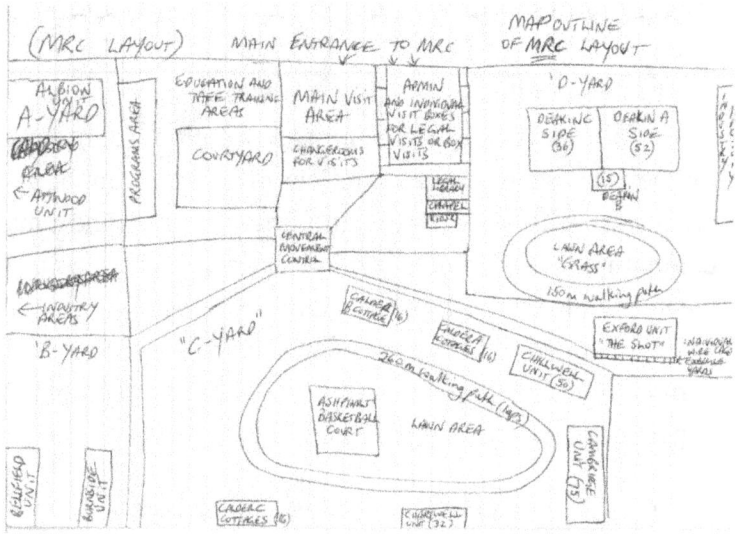

Sirius Unit at Port Phillip Prison

The Sirius Unit at Port Phillip was about 30 metres long by about 20 metres and housed about 60 prisoners, from memory. It was largely full of absolute scum bags and rapists and child molesters and paedophiles. I spent some time there as a transition between Units due to a lack of prison space and cells, and it was disgusting being surrounded by the scum in there.

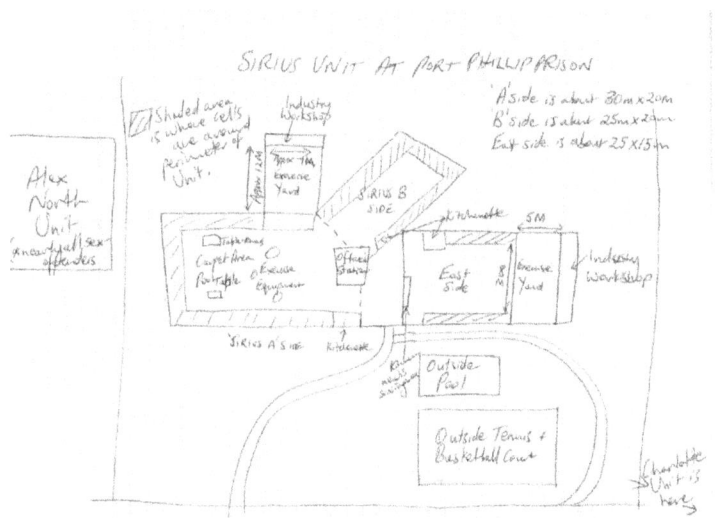

Sketch of 'The Spine'

The Spine refers to the dungeon in Charlotte section at Port Phillip Prison. Charlotte is basically what people would know as 'The Slot' or solitary confinement. However, sometimes what they did at Port Phillip Prison is they would put you in The Spine for a few days or even longer, just to 'break' you even further, before they put you into The Slot (Charlotte).

Charlotte was 22 Hour Lockdown every day, and you were allowed 2 hours in the exercise yard which was an area of cage that was about 6 metres x 3 metres approximately. Most of the time you were there on your own during the 2 hours exercise, but sometimes you had to share it with others. It was very dangerous. At one stage I was sharing my 2 hours exercise time with 2 convicted murderers who had both killed someone in jail!

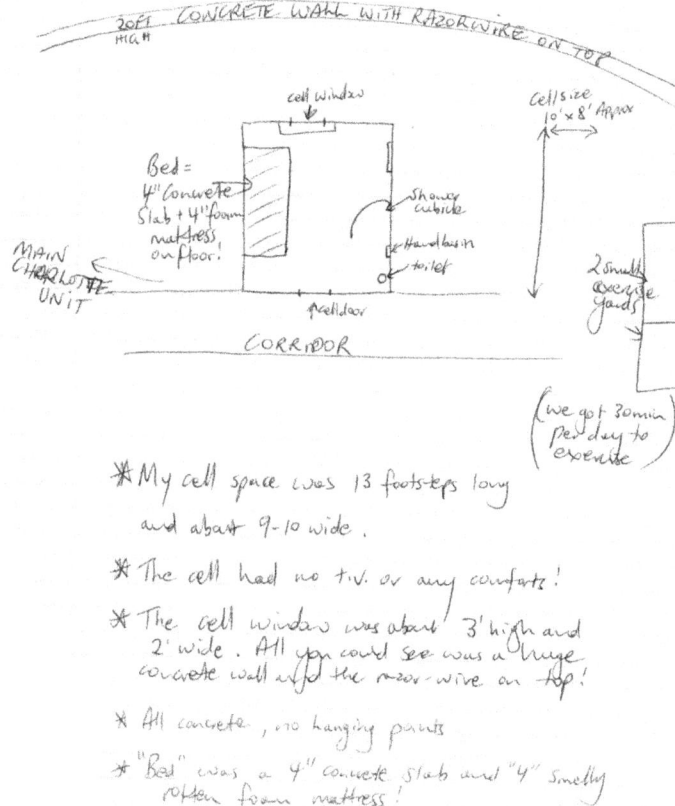

* My cell space was 13 footsteps long and about 9-10 wide.
* The cell had no t.v. or any comforts!
* The cell window was about 3' high and 2' wide. All you could see was a huge concrete wall with the razor-wire on top!
* All concrete, no hanging points
* "Bed" was a 4" concrete slab and "4" smelly rotten foam mattress!

Intel Notes

These refer to conversations that I had with Anthony Dutton about his murder of an innocent victim (Angelique). They clearly show and provide an accurate account of the specific details about the murder, how he did it, what he used, what happened during the struggle, and what she was wearing, and a total lack of empathy and remorse on his part. He kept saying that he loved her, but he clearly planned and orchestrated this murder. He then tried to pretend he wanted to take an overdose and commit suicide. * More importantly, those specific details could not have possibly been known by anyone else but the perpetrator.

/ Court Notes 1.

Ron Baker was Managing Director of Harris Scarfe in the early 80's. He left the company and returned back to Harris Scarfe in 94.

Ron Baker - 0411.224.185
Lyn Baker - 0411.224.187

When Ron Baker came back to H/S in 94, he brought his wife also into the company as Marketing Manager.

Ron and Lyn purchased an old home at Nth Adelaide in approx 94/95. Tony went to the auction with Ron + Lyn, but they purchased the house after auction (bidding never reached the Reserve).

Ron + Lyn told Tony that they didn't want to move into the house until it was fully renovated. And Ron told Tony that didn't want to see any renovation costs on his H/S account, and didn't expect any bills for works done. * Lyn was to supervise the renovations, picking colours, kitchen design, and carpets.

Lyn told Tony to make sure Ron never read any accounts for works done. Tony spoke to Ron about this and Ron told him "Tony, just bury the costs where they can't be found,..." he suggested in the "Stores" expansion.

Ron said at one stage that I was to make sure it's all lost, so that we don't end up with another Coles-Myer saga", even though alot of work had already been done when the Coles-Myer saga came to light.

Tues 5/12 lockdown — Debbie Fetter

- Can't understand why he did it. ("loss")
- couldn't kill someone
- didn't worry about consequences re his mum, his business, his car, his clothes & woke etc because he thought he'd be dead! suicide
- he can't handle "loss"
- next

- Debbie Fetter — organised Year 2000 New Year celebration
                    — 2 years with mate
- when she got rid of him in Oct 2000 he was shattered "loss"

- Saw a Psychologist — she told him Debbie tried to give him tips/hints

Tony didn't suspect anything {
  ① affair with boss at Bundaberg
  ② new clothes in wardrobe (he had bought these)
  ③ $4,000 paid off on her credit card etc.
}

5/12⁴

maybe an hour or so... I just did it...

Q. Do you want to stop Tony?... why not stop... do you want to give it a rest?

A - No I need to talk about it... I just lost it, I cracked... I got the knife from the kitchen and I hit her in the face with it ... on the left I think ... her neck ... she woke up and I punched her! She said "Stop it, stop it, you're killing me"... I stabbed her again ... ... paused. ... we wrestled and we fell on the floor ... I had to kill her ... she grabbed the knife and stabbed me

I grabbed that cord, the lamp cord thing... white ... I strangled her from behind ... I wouldn't let go ...

Q What then, was that it? A - No I hit her with the lamp .... and .... paused ....

Q - And what then ... you took the pills..?? (was that it?)

A - No ... the hammer ... I hit her with that too! I hit her with the hammer ... I think I did....

Q Jesus Tony ... I can't believe this?

5/12

~~[scribble]~~ hammer ~~[scribble]~~ hammer found on her body.
— Yes - I hit her with it.

computer on kitchen table

✓ Red computer on kitchen table. Answer is in "personals" (file)

"in personals"

lots of emails of Ange
lots of emails of Angelique's

✓ Thought it would be disaster
Q: what were you thinking would happen?
A: I thought it would be a disaster.

✓ Frightened she was seeing someone else — [I was frightened she was seeing someone else.]

✓ Q: Did you take tablets first or text first?
A: Tablets first, and then text sms
Sue Alan Thomas   to Alan Thomas (Shopfitter)
Denby Lewis   Denby Lewis
Cathy   Cathy   + ?

160

5/12

~~room~~ dark (room was dark)
~~venetian~~ blinds on sliding door
~~going~~ to patio — there are venetian blinds
on the sliding door going out
to patio. They were shut.
Hence dark.

~~had~~ discussed suicide couple weeks
~~earlier~~ Have you ever discussed suicide with Angelique
before? Yes, about 2 weeks ago.

(She said ~~don't~~ "Don't be stupid Tony")
" She said don't be stupid Tony"

16/6 "wait for you at the Rock"
→ Note dated 16/6/2006 — Angelique wrote how much
  she loved me & said she'd
  meet me or "wait for you
  at the 'Rock'"

~~day~~

pyjamas   blue + white
                long ones

made love 9pm
sleep 10pm

went to kitchen for knife
She not wake up.

2 wooden knife blocks in
            kitchen

6" long

I think bakelite (type)

" hit her in the face with it"

contemplated 10 min

Blue + white pyjamas — silky long

9 o'clock bed

made love

10 o'clock sleep

6" long
bakelite
I o— in contemplate

Q — Where did you stab her?
- Stabbed her in the face / left cheek / neck?
- also in the neck / upper chest
- don't know how many times
- she woke up + said
- she said Stop it, stop it (you're killing me)
- She fought me, we rolled onto floor, she took knife from me
- she stabbed me twice I think / leg I think
- she then threw knife under the bed / ? little table
- not long after that I strangled her with the lamp cord / hit her with lamp.
* where were you on floor? b/w bed + ensuite ?
- Q You Strugled? Yeah

- She didn't make
- used his R/H
- hit her in the face with knife
- ~~I think~~ thinks she bit him on Right hand
- whole knife struck her in face!
- impact left cheek!!
- then she woke up + they
- rolled on floor for awhile
- + she stabbed me in the leg

Sms message — "Both dead. Look on red computer under "personal".

Wed 6/12

1.

Tony had 1 own visit with Anthony Mapee. He came back a bit stressed because he was told his mum was coming for Xmas to visit him next week! He was stressed.

11.59 Count dave and Tony wanted to chat. He started feeling sorry for himself with "What have I done to myself?" "How could I do this to myself?" etc. "But I didn't think it would be a problem I never thought I needed to worry about these things... the consequences... I thought I was going to die... I tried to kill myself!"

I said "You can't think like that Tony"

Tony then said "Maybe I shouldn't have text Coffey and Alan... I should have just left it... then I'd be dead... we'd be together on the "Rock". I knew she was dead... it was a disaster... just like I thought But I stuffed up! I shouldn't have sent the text!!

Q. Tony, once you killed Angelique, did you just got get the pills, and then you text didn't you... that's right?

A - Tony said "Yeah I took the pills, I knew the answers were on the red computer"

Q. Where was the computer Tony? Was that....

A - On the kitchen table... if was on, I remember it was on. The stuff was all there, in the "Personals"

Q What sort of stuff Tony?
A - Everything, it's all there, the cops have got it

6/12 2

now. My Samsung laptop, the red one. It's all there.

Q. Tony, I'm confused... I have to be honest.. I can't understand why you did it.

A - I loved her so much. I loved her. Do you know what I mean? I just thought, she wanted to leave me and she was out with others ... I know that ... all the text + stuff... deleting them late at night... her were others and I couldn't handle it .. I cracked!!

Q What, you mean you were jealous?

A - Yeah... I suppose, I couldn't stand the thought of losing her,.... I'd already lost Debbie ... I couldn't let that happen again!! I had to kill her ... I had to .. I loved her too much.

※ We were interrupted by lunch call. So we stopped chatting for now. I suggested he see if he can get an appointment with the psychiatrist for a chat because he was getting very angry & depressed!

Wed 6/12 2/7/13 Elizabeth
18/7/46 Tony

pt'd — "I love your fluid taste."

p316 Renby email 23/6/06

D+C Design + Construction S/C
Level 2 /19 Cato St

pt/hrs
ph 9804-3944
fax 9804-3534
0407 975 985

White cloudy liquid in bathroom

Samsung R30 laptop computer
Model NP-Q30T002/SAU

(Diazepam based tablet Valium
Knife under bed)

3.

Renovations consisted of

- Demolition of Interior walls — Joe Za Za
- Hard Plastering — " " "
- New Ceilings & Cornices — Steve Clark
- Renovated Bathroom — Joe Za Za
- New Kitchen — John Gleeson
- New Built in Robes — " "
- New Air Conditioning — (FHP Air Conditioning)
- Re-wiring of Electrical — Mark Johns
- New Floor Coverings — Ron Van Andren Carpets
- New Roof — Morgan Plumbing
- New Plumbing — " "
- Upgrade Garage — Carpenter
- Upgrade Cellar — "
- Carpentry including new doors — "
- Landscaping / Paving — Joe Za Za / Bob Simpson
- Renovations to Front Fence — Joe Za Za
- Painting entire Inside + Outside — Johnny Haines

※ All these Tradies knew they were doing work, and that the costs would be "lost" within the Company on "Stores" expansions.

5/12

her... She didn't love Dean....

Q You told me that she was leaving you for Dean, you told me that's why you decided to kill her. Isn't that what you told me? I'm sure that's what you've told me??

A Tony said "Yeah... but it was more the other stuff... Tosh, Phil... I just couldn't stand it anymore... and I guess... I was so bloody stressed with the business and with her.... I loved her and felt like,... I thought she was going to leave me... I couldn't stand it..."

Q So you decided to kill her?.... When was that? You said to me once,.... that you decided about a week or two before that night." Is that right?

A Tony – Yeah, I didn't know when or what, but I just knew I had to do it. And that night I just cracked... her argument, the phone call with Subway... I just lost it.... that was it..... So we went home.... we made love and ..... paused....

Q. So was this in the middle of the night or what?

A. Nah, we went to bed early... around 9 o'clock I think.... we made love and I loved her so much... I wanted her to fall asleep.... pause.... then I don't know

1/12/06

✓ electrical cord found near her → he used that to strangle her — white I think
✓ lamp bedside table lamp found near her
✓ - strangled her from behind
✓ lampshade broken → he hit her with it after he strangled her → why → to make sure she's dead

☆ cops found a hammer on her (s) → Tony said he hit her with it
— killed her because he loved her!!

a computer/emails/etc. Angelique's emails on computer.

Port Phillip Shopping List

This is the Canteen Shopping List that shows the types of groceries and other items that prisoners could access and purchase at the time, when they were in prison. It also shows the costs for each item.

Each prisoner could access these once a week, as long as they had the money. Prisoners could earn $5 a day by working in prison, or a little more if they were working in more important jobs like in the kitchen.

The shopping list is on the next two pages.

Port Phillip Prison Shop Catalog

PORT PHILLIP PRISON SHOP - PRICE LIST

Product	Description/Comments	Code	Price
white ox large		2003	$23.10
drum large		2002	$23.10
white ox small		2014	$14.10
peter jack virginia		2010	$11.95
peter jack extra		2008	$11.95
peter jack super		2009	$10.55
winfield red		2006	$11.95
winfield blue		2005	$10.70
cigarette papers		2001	$0.37
cigarette filters		2016	$1.05
matches	maximum 10	2012	$0.12
aerogard		7024	$4.95
aerogramme	overseas letter	6006	$1.00
after shave		1046	$5.72
air freshner		1030	$1.65
anchovies		4029	$2.30
apricots dried		7020	$2.50
assorted biscuits		4034	$3.47
assorted creams		4035	$3.95
baked beans heinz		4007	$1.10
bakedbeans		4006	$0.85
battery AA		6007	$1.20
battery AAA		6022	$1.20
bbq shapes		4031	$2.08
beef noodles		4024	$0.60
bounty		3011	$1.10
braised steak		7052	$2.75
bran		4057	$0.55
butter menthols		3009	$1.00
cake	rich fruit cake	7001	$3.74
calculator		6008	$8.80
can opener		4050	$2.00
card birthday	please specify age and gender	6016	$0.99
cards blank	specify occasion	6021	$0.99
cards valentine		7014	$1.50
cassette tape	90 min	6031	$2.31
cheese	laughing cow	4061	$2.25
cherry ripe		3003	$1.00
chicken noodles		4023	$0.60
chilli flakes		4043	$1.05
chilli sauce	please specify hot or sweet	4065	$2.90
chips	copper kettle	3016	$1.00
chips chicken		3017	$0.85
chips salt&vinegar		3018	$0.85
chocolate	cadbury dairy milk	3010	$2.20
chocolate	cadbury fruit and nut	3027	$2.20
clipboard		6036	$2.64
coconut milk		4012	$1.75
coffee	intrenational roast	4041	$3.70
coffee bags		4097	$2.70
coffee maker		6042	$7.70

174

Port Phillip Prison Shop Catalog

PORT PHILLIP PRISON SHOP - PRICE LIST

Product	Description/Comments	Code	Price
coffee mio	pluger coffee	4075	$3.75
colgate	toothpaste	1038	$2.09
comb		1006	$0.35
computer disk 3.5		6033	$0.83
condensed milk	can	4048	$1.95
conditioner		1057	$1.85
conditioner	at present pears	1056	$2.85
cordial orange	750ml	5004	$1.65
cordial raspberry	750ml	5001	$1.65
cotton buds	200	1027	$2.50
cross & chain		6035	$6.05
deodorant gillette	gillette	7015	$2.99
cup of soup	beef	4019	$1.60
cup of soup	chicken	4021	$1.60
cup of soup	tomato	4020	$1.60
curry		4066	$1.05
cutlery	knife, fork, teaspoon & spoon	777	$3.50
dental floss		1013	$3.19
deodorant	revenge	1029	$2.50
diet cordial	750ml	5020	$1.65
dry ginger	1.25	7049	$1.10
eggs	one dozen	4055	$2.70
electric kettle		7040	$14.30
envelope plain		6003	$0.04
envelope stamped		6005	$0.60
envelopeA4	A4 SIZE	7031	$0.15
eraser		7055	$1.00
exercise book	64 pages	6024	$0.55
face wash	antibacterial solution	1036	$8.40
fan		6044	$27.50
flavored tea		7061	$3.30
fried dace		7019	$1.80
fruit salad		4027	$1.85
garlic		4085	$1.05
ginger		4084	$1.05
glue		6027	$5.50
grated cheese		4063	$1.70
hair brush		1005	$1.76
hair tie		1022	$0.10
hand lotion	vaseline intensive care	1035	$4.04
highlighters	please specify colour	7058	$1.20
honey		4038	$4.45
hot noodles		7018	$0.60
jelly beans		7013	$2.00
kellogs	8 varieties small packets	4098	$4.70
kidney beans		4037	$1.25
kit kat		3006	$1.00
kraft cheese	chunky	4061	$2.25

Prison Shop List

Page 2

175

Prisoner Canteen Order Form

This is the prisoner's meal list and where they can order their meals for a week at a time. As you can see, they had a choice of Vegetarian or Healthy meals as well.

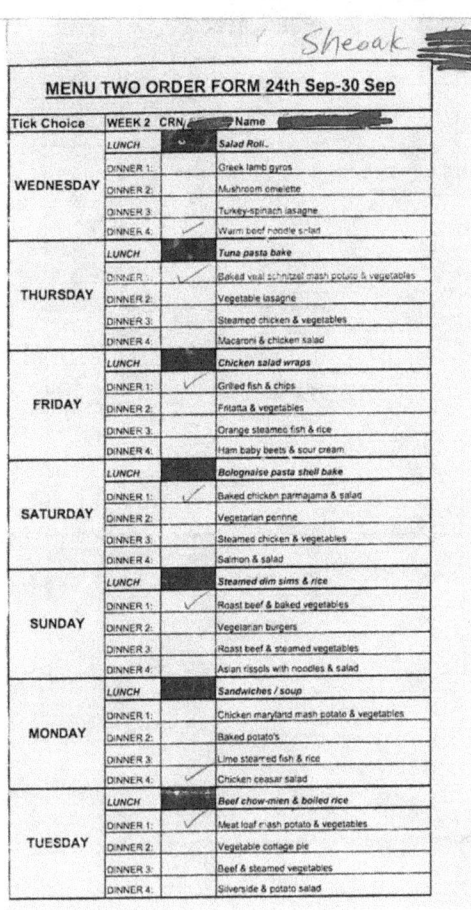

Prisoner Canteen Shop Receipt

This is the receipt every prisoner gets when they do their weekly shop, but then they get a receipt which clearly shows them what balance they have left and what items they bought.

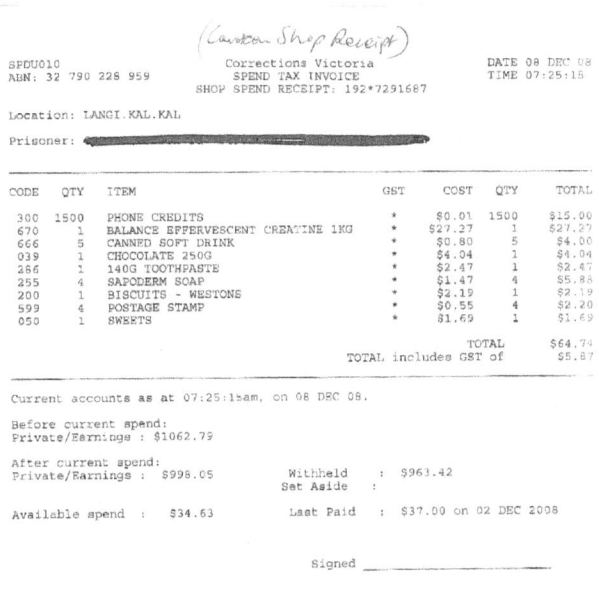

```
SPDU010                    (Canteen Shop Receipt)
ABN: 32 790 228 959          Corrections Victoria           DATE 08 DEC 08
                             SPEND TAX INVOICE              TIME 07:25:15
                      SHOP SPEND RECEIPT: 192*7291687

Location: LANGI.KAL.KAL

Prisoner: ▓▓▓▓▓▓▓▓▓▓▓▓▓▓▓▓▓▓▓▓▓▓▓▓▓▓▓▓▓▓

CODE   QTY    ITEM                               GST    COST    QTY    TOTAL

300    1500   PHONE CREDITS                      *      $0.01   1500   $15.00
670    1      BALANCE EFFERVESCENT CREATINE 1KG  *      $27.27  1      $27.27
666    5      CANNED SOFT DRINK                  *      $0.80   5      $4.00
039    1      CHOCOLATE 250G                     *      $4.04   1      $4.04
266    1      140G TOOTHPASTE                    *      $2.47   1      $2.47
255    4      SAPODERM SOAP                      *      $1.47   4      $5.88
200    1      BISCUITS - WESTONS                 *      $2.19   1      $2.19
599    4      POSTAGE STAMP                      *      $0.55   4      $2.20
050    1      SWEETS                             *      $1.69   1      $1.69
                                                               TOTAL   $64.74
                                             TOTAL includes GST of     $5.87

Current accounts as at 07:25:15am, on 08 DEC 08.

Before current spend:
Private/Earnings : $1062.79

After current spend:
Private/Earnings : $998.05      Withheld   : $963.42
                                Set Aside  :

Available spend  : $34.63       Last Paid  : $37.00 on 02 DEC 2008

                                Signed _____
```

This is an actual real copy of the weekly shopping list for this particular inmate. Each inmate is allowed to spend some money once a week for their so-called "goodies" and this can be anything from snacks, toiletries, tobacco or just about anything else.
  • This

Song – Take It Back

This was a song that I wrote the lyrics for, on the inside, and I got another prisoner to do the melody or the score.

```
TAKE IT BACK                                              14-JUL-08
Intro   Am / / /  Em / / /  Am / / /  Em / / /

Verse 1:
Am                       Em                    Am
TAKE IT BACK,     TAKE IT ALL BACK NOW...   THE THINGS I GAVE
Em               G          Am
LIKE THE TAST OF MY KISS ON YOUR LIPS
Am                    Em                    Am
I MISS THAT NOW,   I CAN'T TRY ANY HARDER   THAN I DO...
Em            G             Am              G       Am        G
ALL THE REASONS I GAVE EXCUSES I MADE      FOR YOU...   ARE BROKEN IN TWO

Chorus:
Dm                          Gm7
ALL THE THINGS LEFT UNDISCOVERED
Dm                               Gm7
LEAVE ME WAITING AND LEFT TO WONDER
F                A7
ALL THE THINGS I'VE LEFT UNDISCOVERED
Dm                         Gm7
LEAVE ME EMPTY AND LEFT TO WONDER
F            A7
I NEED YOU,   YEAH I NEED YOU
Dm              F       G      Am     F    G    Am   Em   Am   Em
DON'T WALK AWAY,   PLEASE COME AND STAY

Verse 2:
Am                    Em                    Am
TOUCH ME NOW,     HOW I WANNA FEEL...   SOMETHING SO REAL
Em             G          Am
PLEASE REMIND ME,   MY LOVE
Am                       Em                   Am
PLEASE TAKE ME BACK,  I CAN'T FAKE IT    I CAN'T HATE...
Em           G          Am     G     Am          G
BUT IT'S MY HEART THAT'S ABOUT TO BREAK, I'M NOT BREATHING

Chorus:
Dm                          Gm7
ALL THE THINGS LEFT UNDISCOVERED
Dm                               Gm7
LEAVE ME WAITING AND LEFT TO WONDER
F                A7
ALL THE THINGS I'VE LEFT UNDISCOVERED
Dm                         Gm7
LEAVE ME EMPTY AND LEFT TO WONDER
F            A7
I NEED YOU,   YEAH I NEED YOU
Dm              F       G      Am     F    G
DON'T WALK AWAY,   PLEASE COME AND STAY

Am                        Em                   Am
WHEN I'M IN THE DARK,   AND ALL ALONE       MY HEART IS HURTING...
Em            G              Am       G       Am  G
ALL MY TROUBLES THERE AND I CLOSE MY EYES,   I'M ALONE

Chorus:
Dm                          Gm7
ALL THE THINGS LEFT UNDISCOVERED
Dm                               Gm7
LEAVE ME WAITING AND LEFT TO WONDER
F                A7
ALL THE THINGS I'VE LEFT UNDISCOVERED
Dm                         Gm7
LEAVE ME EMPTY AND LEFT TO WONDER
F            A7
I NEED YOU,   YEAH I NEED YOU
Dm              F       G      Am     F    G    Am   Em   Am   Em
DON'T WALK AWAY,   PLEASE COME AND STAY

Take It Back (A).doc
```

www.ingramcontent.com/pod-product-compliance
Lightning Source LLC
Chambersburg PA
CBHW051549020426
42333CB00016B/2175